Too Broken to be Fixed?

Too Broken to Be Fixed?

A Spiritual Guide to Inner Healing

Gloria Morrow, Ph.D.

Shining Glory Publications,
Inc. Pomona, California

Published by Shining Glory Publications, Inc.
2249 North Garey Avenue
Pomona, California 91767
(909) 392-6907

Notice: The information in this book is true and complete to the best of the author and
publisher's knowledge. However, the names, and other pertinent details concerning
individuals in this book have been changed. This book is intended only as an information reference and should not replace, countermand, or conflict with the advice
given to readers by their professional mental health providers, and/or physicians. It is
sold with the understanding that the author and publisher are not engaged in
rendering medical, mental health, psychological, or any other kind of personal or
professional services in the book. The reader should consult her or his culturally
competent med-ical and/or mental health professional before adopting any of the
suggestions in this book or drawing inferences from it. The author and publisher
disclaim all liability in connection with the specific personal use of any and all
information provided in this book.

Morrow, Gloria, 1950-
        Too broken to be fixed? A spiritual guide to inner healing /by Gloria Morrow.
– 1st ed. p.cm.

Includes bibliographical references and index

ISBN-13: 978-1981279333

ISBN-10: 1981279334

Printed and bound in the United States of America

This book is dedicated to my beloved husband,
Reverend Tommy Morrow.
You always see more in me than I ever see in myself.
This walk of faith would have been much more difficult
without your love, encouragement, and support.

Too Broken to be Fixed?

CONTENTS

ACKNOWLEDGMENTS

This project has been a work in progress for the past three years, and it would still be in the dream stage without the generous love, friendship, and support of so many wonderful people. I would first like to acknowledge the individuals who have contributed to my growth and development as a scholar and practitioner. The mentoring and support I have received from each of you have enabled me to use my gifts and talents to serve the community I love and respect. Special thanks to Dr. Nolan Penn, Dr. Rodney Davis, Dr. Fran Rockwell, Dr. Judith Schonholtz-Reed, Dr. Nancy Goldberger, and Dr. Aghop Der Karabetian, for encouraging me to write long before this book idea reached maturity.

I would like to thank my clients for allowing me to learn from you. You have entrusted me with your care, and I will never do anything to compromise your trust. Your experiences have been pivotal to many of the themes captured in this book. Furthermore, your stories may help those who avoid seeking help, because they feel all alone in their struggle. While your stories are told in such a way as to protect your identity, the essence of your courage and strength is greatly felt and admired.

This project would have been an impossible feat without the editorial skills and support of Tammi Phillips, Joann Washington,

Doretha Johnson, and Emily Newell. Thank you for your major contribution to this work.

To my colleagues, thank you for helping me to believe that I had something important to say. I am especially grateful to Dr. Jose Cervantes, Attorney Latonya Slack, and Reverend William E. Tyler for your generous remarks. Rev. Tyler, I must say your willingness to open the dialogue surrounding depression and suicide in your church has been a valuable asset to this book. Thank you for daring to tread in unsettled waters. You are certainly a great role model for other pastors as they seek ways to promote total health and wellness for their parish-ioners.

To all of the community organizations whose mission it is to enhance the mental and physical well being of African Americans, such as California Black Women's Health Project (Attorney Latonya Slack and Attorney Crystal Crawford), Prototypes Black Infant Health (Ms. Stacy Powell and Attorney Lee Brown Rafe, Partners in Faith (PIF), and my research colleagues, Myriam Aragon, Dr. Glenn Gamst, Dr. Leticia Arellano, Dr. Robin Huff-Musgrove, Dr. Aghop Der Karabetian, and Dr. Richard Dana, thank you for your commitment to the community. Our collaboration has certainly been fruitful in helping to crystallize some of the thoughts and ideas that are reflected in this book.

To my church family, Victory Community Church, thank you for all the love and kindness you always extend to me. I am proud to represent you. To my community, thank you for reminding me why I am here.

To Doris Green, Olivia Wise, Shirley Edmond, Emily & Guy Newell, Annie Washington, Ron & Doretha Johnson, Josie Satterfield,

Ann Wichman, Donna & Gary George, Valerie Jordan, and Jessie Brooks, thank you for your endless love and support. When I thought I was too broken to be fixed, your love paved the way for my inner healing.

To my special adopted daughters and mentees, LaNicia Williams, Rochelle Phillips, Joann Washington, Joella Washington, Lillie Frierson, Arnisha Morrow, Pamela Beeks, Sandra Barrow, Maria Salas, Myesha Taylor, and Rob'n Lewis, it is my prayer that something in this book will encourage you to pick up the mantle and carry the work forward, long after I'm gone. The work must continue!

This labor of love would have been impossible without the love and support of family, who not only provided emotional support, but some of you rolled up your sleeves and contributed time and money to this project. To Dr. Murray and Annie Lois Morrow, thank you for believing in me and serving as true role models, mentors and confidants.

To my beloved siblings, Charlie Powell, Pastor Gwendolyn Phillips Coates, Harold Wayne Phillips, Randy Cornell Phillips, your spouses, and my nieces and nephews, thank you for allowing me to be me. Knowing you are proud of me has served as a valuable source of motivation for me.

To my precious mom and dad, Reverend Harold and Henrietta Phillips, you have truly been an inspiration to me. As I sit with clients who did not have the opportunity to grow up with the love you demonstrated to me on a daily basis, I feel extremely blessed. Thank you for continually reminding me that I am loved and wanted.

To my grandchildren, MaLaun Alexandria Phillips, Kalin Alexander Phillips, Dakari Veals, and my adopted granddaughter,

Siannah Hudson, you are the joy of my life, and prayerfully the work I am doing now will make the world a better place for you to live in.

To my children, Steven, Sharmika, TaMia, and TaLese, thank you for loving me enough to share me with others. Steve, you are extraordinarily gifted, and it is truly a blessing that your talents have been used to assist me with this project. However, I am even more excited because you too have been gifted to bind up the broken hearted, and I know you will continue to use your gifts. Sharmika, you are a blessing in my life, and I thank God for you. TaMia and TaLese, you are bright, beautiful, and intelligent young ladies. I can hardly wait to see the great things you will do with your lives. I pray that this book will bless you for years to come.

Last, but certainly not least, to Tommy, my husband and friend, you are the love of my life and my private motivator. Thank you for giving me the freedom to become all God wants me to become. When I wanted to quit you would not let me, so thank you for saving me from myself. I love you.

To God be the glory for the great things He has done!

INTRODUCTION

"I wish I was dead!" Do you ever remember saying those words as a child when things weren't going your way? Well, I do, and my mother never took me seriously. I can still hear her stern words, *"I can make your wish come true if you ever say something silly like that again."* That was it. So much for self-expression! Unfortunately, far too often people silently wish they were dead, and even if they were to say it out loud, some would not take them seriously. In fact, we still have a hard time believing that Black folk would consider harming themselves. But that is not always the case. African Americans do commit suicide because they can no longer cope with the painful symptoms of depression. That's right, despite the myth, Black people do suffer from depression, and sometimes we can't just snap out of it as we are often encouraged to do. The case of Frank will underscore the need for depression to be taken seriously and treated in the Black community, which is the essence of this book.

The last time I saw Frank alive, he was bubbly and full of life as he shared plans of an anticipated bright and promising future. It was three years ago, that my husband and I met Frank and his wife Sandra at a social function. Even though this was our first meeting, I could tell that Frank loved to make people laugh. According to the friend that introduced us, Frank was on his way to becoming the next great Christian comic. He and Sandra had been married twenty-five years, and the couple had two beautiful children. I thought to myself, what a wonderful family. We all had a good time at the party, and exchanged telephone numbers so we could get together again. But our plans were interrupted.

While sitting in my office a few weeks later, I received a telephone call that really changed my life; Frank committed suicide. I learned that he waited for his family to leave the family home, pulled out a gun, and shot himself in the head. I, like many of those who knew him better, were shocked by the news. The friend that introduced us was devastated, and she asked me a barrage of questions, including: *(1) Why would this seemingly well rounded, happy, and psychologically hardy man do such a thing to himself?; (2) How could he leave his wife and children alone to deal with this senseless tragedy?; and (3) How could a Christian kill himself knowing he may not go to heaven?* I decided to share the clinical explanations to enable her to understand more about the disease that contributes to suicidal behavior, especially after learning that Frank suffered from Bipolar Disorder.

Bipolar Disorder is a form of depression that affects 2.3 million adults in our country. According to the *National Alliance for the Mentally Ill*, Bipolar Disorder is characterized by alternating episodes of mania and depression that can last from days to months. According to the 1994 *DSM-IV* (Diagnostic and Statistical Manual of Mental Disorders, Fourth Edition), individuals suffering from Bipolar Disorder experience some or all of the following symptoms:

Symptoms of Bipolar Disorder

- Inflated self-esteem or grandiosity;
- Decreased need for sleep
- More talkative;
- Flight of ideas or racing thoughts;
- Distractibility;
- Excessive involvement in pleasurable activities resulting in painful consequences, such as excessive spending, irresponsible sexual behavior, or foolish business ventures;
- Suicidal ideation.

People with bipolar disorder (also called manics) tend to display mania (an elevated, euphoric, expansive, or irritable mood) with or without a period of depression. When manics are up, they tend to be cheerful and excitable, and they exhibit behaviors, such as excessive shopping and spending. However, when manics are down, it is difficult for them to get out of bed. It is as if the bottom has dropped out of their world. During the downward spiral, manics become preoccupied with suicidal thoughts, but interestingly enough, they tend to carry those thoughts out when they are on the upward swing because while down, they usually do not have sufficient energy to carry their plans out.

Frank had been in and out of the hospital because of thoughts of killing himself, as well as two prior attempts, but somehow he managed to hide his problems from the outside world, including the church where he was an active and faithful member. He was referred to several therapists and was prescribed an antidepressant by a psychiatrist; however, he failed to attend therapy sessions and refused to take the medication because of his reliance on God for his complete healing. Frank felt that traditional psychological help was incompatible with his belief system, so his condition continued to deteriorate. His depression negatively impacted his life, including his marriage.

It is not uncommon for couples to experience problems in their marital relationship when one or both partners suffer from mental illness. Frank and Sandra were surely no exception, for they had a lot of problems in their marriage. Sandra described Frank as a risk taker, and she believed he put their family at risk of losing everything because of his work instability and the various business ventures he attempted without adequate capital. Manics talk excessively, try to complete 50 things at one time, and spend a lot of money, even if they do not have the money to spend. Frank was driving his wife insane because of his erratic behavior.

Without consistent treatment including medication, the classic bipolar can easily become nasty and cruel when they feel threatened. Sandra confirmed this finding, and stated that Frank could become quite agitated and angry at times. Since Frank did not take his medication as prescribed, he also complained of hearing voices, which is a symptom of the disease. Sandra was becoming more and more frightened of his bizarre behavior, and since she never participated in his treatment, she did not know how to help him nor herself. Now Frank was gone, leaving Sandra with so many unanswered questions.

I felt drawn to this family, partly because of our initial meeting, but mostly because I was looking for answers surrounding African Americans' attitudes and beliefs about mental illness, and why some in our community fail to seek help for psychological and emotional problems. So even though I did not know Frank and his family very well, I decided to attend his funeral. I was hoping to learn something about Frank and his life, as well as to gain a better understanding of why some of our people con-tinue to live in a state of brokenness when help is available. Furthermore, I was very interested in how the church would handle this complex issue.

During the funeral services, the pastor, much to my surprise and delight, did not try to hide the fact that Frank had a psychological problem that caused him to commit suicide. The pastor used this tragedy to teach his people about the impact of mental illness on the household of faith. He further answered the question that I am sure was on the minds of some in attendance: *Is Frank going to hell because he committed suicide?* In response to that silent question, the pastor reassured the congregation by stating: *"If Frank was a Christian, then he has gone to heaven."* Many Christians are under the impression that suicide is an unforgivable sin, and those who commit that sin will be lost forever.

While this thinking may serve as a wonderful deterrent to suicidal behavior among Christians, it may also serve as a difficult issue for family members to deal with when their loved one has committed suicide. There is a sense of unrest for these families when they believe their loved one ended her or his life, without the possibility of going to heaven.

I felt a sense of relief that this pastor appeared to be balanced in his thinking, and then he did another truly insightful and amazing thing. The pastor asked a very important question: *"How many of you in the audience have contemplated taking your own life?"* Initially, I wasn't sure where he was going with this question, but once again, he did not disappoint me. I waited in anticipation to see how the crowd of more than 1000 people would respond to such a personal question. A hush came over the church for what seemed like minutes. I could faintly hear the sweet sounds of the organ, as I began to scan the sizeable audience. Then it happened! Hands began to pop up all over the building. Even I was amazed at the number of people who raised their hands in response to the pastor's provocative question.

I was struck by the pastor's sensitivity to the issue, and his unwillingness to ignore the cause of Frank's death. But I could not help but wonder; if the question had not been asked, would the respondents have continued to remain in silence? Two even more complex questions immediately arose in my mind: *"What would become of those who dared to be honest?"* and *"Were any of the brave respondents in need of treatment and not getting it?"* I was very impressed with the pastor's ingenuity, and I was convinced that he would make sure his parishioners would no longer have to suffer in silence, or feel there was no solution for their brokenness. But I was concerned about those whose pastors lacked the same level of insight and sensitivity.

That day I received further confirmation that our people do suffer from depression, and we do commit suicide. I had an even greater awareness that many of us still suffer in silence by failing to seek help from mental health professionals, which has been discussed by researchers over the past few decades. For example, according to the 1999 *U.S. Surgeon General's Report* on the status of African Americans in the mental health system, we tend to seek mental health treatment at a later stage, have higher drop-out rates, utilize fewer treatment sessions for mental health problems, over utilize inpatient psychiatric care at state hospitals at twice the rate of Whites, and underutilize community mental health services.

In addition, a recent study by the *California Black Women's Health Project* revealed that only 7 percent of African American women suffering from depression were treated, compared to 20 percent of the general population. Furthermore, Black men are usually the last ones to seek help for mental health problems.

There are probably several reasons why some African Americans fail to acknowledge their pain and seek help for it. First, African Americans in this country have been exposed to a long history of racism and discrimination, which continues to plague our community. These experiences and historical events may explain our apprehension about trusting a system that has a history of being discriminatory and unfair to our people. As a result, we have been taught to keep our business to ourselves because we cannot trust the system. Do you remember the famous slogan: *"Whatever is said in this house, stays in this house?"* I certainly do, and if this slogan is implanted in your brain, it may be extremely difficult for you or I to self-disclose or acknowledge pain, which is a necessary first step toward inner healing.

Second, mental illness has traditionally and continues to be a source of stigma for African Americans. One who is viewed as mentally ill in our community is often thought to be crazy and/or weak. To complicate matters, mental illness is not correctly understood by some religious communities, which may make some African Americans feel uncomfortable about seeking mental health services outside their churches, especially if they have been taught that mental illness is a sign that their faith is weak, and/or a penalty for sin.

Third, traditional psychotherapy strategies and techniques are often incompatible with the cultural worldview of some African Americans. Therefore, we may resist seeking help because some therapists may not understand our unique cultural perspective. The three explanations highlighted above will be further explored throughout the pages of this book.

Too Broken to be Fixed? A Spiritual Guide to Inner Healing is intended for broken people, or people who know broken people who need to be healed. This book has been written for both African American females and males because both groups are suffering from untreated depression. This book is also written for mental health professionals of all ethnic/racial/cultural backgrounds who are called to provide mental health services to our unique population. I am hopeful that mental health providers will learn more about the cultural world of African American clients to become better equipped to meet their mental health needs. Finally, this book is written with the African American church and its leaders in mind, to help them to understand more about the mental health needs of the parishioners they serve, and to correct the information that is distributed from pulpits all over the world about mental illness and the role of mental health professionals in helping to repair broken people.

In *Too Broken to be Fixed? A Spiritual Guide to Inner Healing*, you will learn that depression is a disease that is treatable. You will also gain a better understanding about the symptoms of depression, the various explanations of the disease, its lethal impact on everyday life and functioning, and some of the barriers that prevent African Americans from seeking and receiving appropriate help. This book introduces both psychological and spiritual interventions to help broken people to embark upon the road to inner healing. Further, thought provoking activities and comforting scriptures and prayers will be incorporated to help you make it through the chapters of this book, along with real life situations and circumstances to let you know you are not alone.

Too Broken to Be Fixed? A Spiritual Guide to Inner Healing is based on my work as a clinician, academician, researcher, community advocate, and active Christian serving in a leadership role in the local church. The case examples reflect similar situations to those experienced by actual clients, although every effort has been taken to protect the identity of those who have placed their trust in me. I would like to thank the clients, students, church, and community folk who have taught me so much about the mental health needs as well as the strengths of our community.

It is my sincere desire that *Too Broken to be Fixed? A Spiritual Guide to Inner Healing* will pave the way for African American men and women to receive inner healing. We will never be completely rid of brokenness because we are not perfect, nor do we live in a perfect world. In addition, the people we must encounter on a daily basis are not perfect either. Life is unpredictable, and it will take its toll on all of us; however, when we gain the necessary tools to live a healthier life, we are obligated to seize the opportunity to change our destiny, and the destiny of those around us. Please remember, you may be broken, but you are never too broken to be fixed.

CHAPTER ONE
BROKEN, WHO ME?

Acknowledging the Pain

"How are you today? Oh, I'm blessed and highly favored." Is that introductory dialogue familiar to you? Well, I hear it all the time, and unfortunately, many people who make that positive declaration feel anything but blessed and highly favored. In fact, some of these folk feel down right miserable, and yet cannot admit that they are in pain. Every living person on this planet, is experiencing, has experienced, or will experience feelings of sadness and pain during his or her lifetime. However, some African Americans not only have a difficult time acknowledging their pain, they fail to seek help for it. When confronted, however, they scream out in protest, **BROKEN, WHO ME? I DON'T THINK SO**.

According to a report in a recent issue of *Psychology Today's Blues Buster Newsletter*, close to 6% of the African American community is affected by depression in any given year. While we do not appear to suffer from depression any more than other ethnic groups, we do seem to have a more difficult time seeking help for the disease as well as other mental and physical disorders. This is particularly troubling because we may be more at risk of experiencing depression and other illnesses because of a variety of issues, such as racism, sexism, ageism, discrimination, racial profiling, terrorism, domestic violence, abuse, divorce, family problems, church problems, and financial problems. These social ills make us sad and angry on the inside, but we sometimes ignore our pain, making us more susceptible to both mental and physical distress. Yet we tend to hide, and suffer in silence.

Nobody Knows But Jesus

Picture Rose, a 48 year-old African American female, as she sits in church, dressed from head to toe, a true picture of wholeness and holiness. She lifts her hands to the Lord when the praise leader requests the congregation to do so, and she cries. When the pastor preaches, she cries. During the altar call and invitational, she is the first to go up for prayer, and she cries. The waiting congregation views Rose as highly Spiritual and connected to God. However, they haven't really looked into her eyes. All they focus on is her outer appearance, which is quite misleading. *Nobody knows the trouble she's seen, nobody knows but Jesus*, and Rose wants to keep it that way. She has silently tucked away her pain and suffering, and she hides, but she will not be able to hide forever. If Rose cannot acknowledge her condition to herself, it certainly will be impossible for her to acknowledge her condition to those who can help her. So she suffers from depression in silence.

Rose said to me during our initial session, *"I thought if I could just get to the church, everything would be all right. I felt good as long as I was sitting there. I would get caught up in the spirit as long as I was there, but when I would leave the church, the spirit seemed to leave too."*

The church is often used like an emergency room, where broken and sick people go for emergency treatment. However, if the church is unable to properly diagnose its patients, or if its patients are not open and honest about their symptoms and pain, those patients in need of repair will only receive temporary relief.

While we may have good reason for keeping our troubles to our-selves, it has not served us well psychologically and physically, and some of us are unhealthy because we live in a state of denial. It is dif-ficult to acknowledge pain when we have become so good at hiding it. We wear a mask, hoping no one will see the hurting person behind the mask. When some of us step out of our beautiful homes, we look like we have it going on, but on the inside we are shattered to pieces with-out a plan for getting healed. We are broken!

What Does it Mean to be Broken?

According to Webster, there are several words used to describe what it means to be "broken:"

Not complete or free
Violently separated into parts
Shattered
Damaged
Fractured
Irregular
Made weak
Interrupted
Crushed
Bankrupt
Cut-off
Disconnected

Brokenness is unavoidable and if allowed to persist without interruption, it can negatively impact every aspect of life. This condition can impair the individual to the point where psychological and medical interventions are imminent. Please know when you or I suffer from emotional distress, physical distress may be waiting in the wings. Brokenness that is ignored will destroy dreams and goals, and everyday existence may become unbearable.

Have you ever had a headache or stomach pain your medical doctor could not explain? If so, chances are you were experiencing emotional or psychological distress. We do not seem to have a difficult time admitting when we are stressed out, because stress is a more acceptable and popular concept; however, it is much more difficult to acknowledge the presence of psychological distress. Nonetheless, brokenness makes one feel empty on the inside, and it does not take long for every relationship (family, friends, community, or work) to be negatively affected by it.

I'm not Broken, I'm Just Mad

Kathy was a most miserable 28 year-old single African American female with a 6 year-old son. She was angry with her baby's daddy, and continued to harbor hatred toward him because of his disapperance act shortly after her son was born. Kathy was left to care for her young child alone. He was unemployed when the baby was born, so needless to say, he never supported the child financially.

Kathy's mother had been deceased since she was 10 years old. Her maternal grandmother, who died when Kathy was 18 years old, raised her and her two siblings. Kathy never knew her father, and she was not very close to her siblings. Therefore, she was virtually alone with a limited support system. Kathy was suffering from a broken heart, which impacted her ability to trust. She had a very negative attitude, and people tried to stay out of her way.

Since Kathy had few family members in her experience, she developed a relationship with an older woman at work. This woman was able to see that Kathy was in trouble and in desperate need of help. But when she attempted to make recommendations to Kathy about seeking counseling, Kathy refused and made statements like, *"There's nothing wrong with me. I am not the problem."* But there was something eating at Kathy from the inside that was about to destroy her life.

Kathy had an anger problem that affected every aspect of her life, including her job. She was always irritable, and she blamed others for her behavior, failing to take responsibility for her own actions. Kathy was written up on several occasions because of her negative disposition. She was withdrawn, and except for the older woman at work, she isolated herself from others. The last time Kathy was written up she was reprimanded and placed on probation. She was also mandated by the court system to participate in an anger management program because of a road rage incident, which led to a misdemeanor criminal charge against her.

While participating in the anger management program, Kathy was referred to me for individual therapy. After a thorough assessment, it was determined that she was suffering from depression that was inter-fering with her daily functioning. For example, Kathy would rather sleep than eat, and it was becoming increasingly difficult for her to get up in the morning. Her son was late for school everyday because of her depression. Every relationship she had was either terminated or extremely strained, because Kathy was a wounded vessel in need of repair. However, nothing changed in her life until she was able to acknowledge her condition. Through weekly therapy sessions, we were able to get to the root of Kathy's anger and begin the process of healing.

FOOD FOR THOUGHT

Kathy's story is an example of what can happen when one ignores one's state of brokenness and fails to seek inner healing. Yes, we are all broken and cracked to one degree or another, but some of us are totally shattered. Since acknowledging your pain is the first step toward inner healing, please take a few minutes to complete the Morrow Brokenness Checklist to begin the process of acknowledging your pain. This checklist is not a scientifically tested instrument at this time, nor is it designed to be a diagnostic tool; rather, this checklist will help you to recognize and confront your condition.

Morrow Brokeness Checklist

	Yes	No	
1.	___	___	Do you cry easily?
2.	___	___	Are your feelings easily hurt?
3.	___	___	Do you become angry easily?
4.	___	___	Do you harbor feelings of guilt?
5.	___	___	Are you a constant worrier?
6.	___	___	Are you a constant complainer?
7.	___	___	Are you fearful?
8.	___	___	Are you preoccupied with feelings of death?
9.	___	___	Do you feel all alone?
10.	___	___	Are you jealous of others?
11.	___	___	Do you think you are always right?
12.	___	___	Do you think others are out to get you?
13.	___	___	Do you think you are ugly?
14.	___	___	Do you think others are smarter than you?
15.	___	___	Do you think you are unlovable?
16.	___	___	Do you think you are a loser?
17.	___	___	Do feelings of sadness ever take over your life?
18.	___	___	Do you ever think of harming yourself or others?
19.	___	___	Are you a gossiping person?
20.	___	___	Do you tell lies or inflate the truth?
21.	___	___	Are you critical of others?
22.	___	___	Are you a constant bragger?
23.	___	___	Do you reject feedback from others by becoming defensive when others try to share feedback with you?
24.	___	___	Do you find it difficult to follow the rules?
25.	___	___	Do you put others down?
26.	___	___	Do you eat too much?
27.	___	___	Do you eat too little?
28.	___	___	Do you forgive others when they do you wrong?
29.	___	___	Do you find it difficult to concentrate?
30.	___	___	Are you a procrastinator?
31.	___	___	Are you perfectionistic?
32.	___	___	Are you extremely hard on yourself?
33.	___	___	Are you a people pleaser?
34.	___	___	Do you have an unhealthy sexual appetite?
35.	___	___	Are you having a dHficult time setting and reaching goals?
36.	___	___	Do you feel like you do not matter?
37.	___	___	Do you have a negative, pessimistic outlook on life?

The interesting thing about this Checklist is that any question that you respond to in the affirmative, may suggest that you are broken in some area. However, the degree to which you are broken can easily be determined through assessment tools that are used by psychologists and other mental health professionals. If you continue to deny your state of bro-kenness, it will certainly lead to greater psychological problems, such as depression. It is not easy to confront our condition, but it is essential to do so if we want to experience true inner healing.

What is Depression?

Depression is a treatable disease that can negatively impact one's mind, body, and spirit. If untreated, symptoms of depression can persist for a long period of time, making those who are suffering from the disease highly at risk of experiencing suicidal thoughts and behaviors. People suffering from depression usually lack energy, and have a difficult time getting out of the bed each day for a prolonged period of time. According to the 1999 *Report of the National Institute of Mental Illness*, depression and anxiety are two of the most common psychological disorders, affecting approximately 19 million adults annually. We sometimes suffer from depression, but do not realize it.

My Sap is Down

African Americans may be suffering from the debilitating disease, but may not define their psychological problems in traditional ways. For example, we may refer to depression as *"having the blues," "being down in the dumps,"* and *"feeling down."* Have you ever heard your mother or grandmother say, *"Girl, my sap is down today."* Those words were not always synonymous with depression, but in some cases, that is exactly what our elders were describing. I remember hearing my aunt speak about her sap being down. When her sap was down, she would usually lie around the house, and her voice even lacked energy. Could she have been suffering from depression? If so, no one knew it, not even her.

Most people will admit to experiencing feelings of sadness and depression at some point in their lives, but symptoms sometimes get normalized and people who feel down and out tend to ignore those feelings. Furthermore, as suggested earlier, when we experience somatic symptoms of depression like headaches and stomach pain, we tend to go to the emergency room for help, and when our doctors cannot find anything wrong and advise us to seek psychological help, we go no further.

In order to understand more about the disease, it is important for you to be able to first make the clear distinction between situational depression and clinical depression, so that when you are seeking help, you will have basic information to assist you in the process.

Situational Depression vs. Clinical Depression

All of us are prone to suffer from situational depression due to life circumstances, such as the death of a family member or friend, divorce or other relationship issues, financial problems, or the loss of a job. However, all of the situations cited above can lead to clinical depression, if depressive symptoms persist. Some of the features and characteristics of the various forms of clinical depression, according to the *National Institute of Mental Health* include the following:

Symptoms of Depression

National Institute of Mental Health- NIMH

- Persistent sad, anxious, or "empty" mood
- Feelings of hopelessness, pessimism
- Feelings of guilt, worthlessness, helplessness
- Loss of interest or pleasure in hobbies and activities that were once enjoyed, including sex
- Decreased energy, fatigue, being "slowed down"
- Difficulty concentrating, remembering, making decisions
- Insomnia, early-morning awakening, or oversleeping
- Appetite and/or weight loss or overeating and weight gain
- Thoughts of death or suicide; suicide attempts
- Restlessness, irritability
- Persistent physical symptoms that do not respond to treatment, such as headaches, digestive disorders, and chronic pain
- Mania
- Abnormal or excessive elation
- Unusual irritability
- Decreased need for sleep
- Grandiose notions
- Increased talking
- Racing thoughts
- Increased sexual desire
- Markedly increased energy
- Poor judgment
- Inappropriate social behavior

African Americans do not always present with some of the more traditional symptoms of depression, such as social withdrawal, unhappiness, or lack of concentration. Rather, some of us tend to experience weight gain due to changes in appetite as opposed to weight loss (especially African American women), fatigue due to insomnia, physical symptoms that are unexplained, and irritability and agitation (Clark, 1998). Individuals suffering from clinical depression are in desperate need of treatment, and failure to receive it may have devastating effects on their personal and professional lives. Sharon's story is an example of the consequences of untreated depression.

God will Fix it

Sharon, a 32 year-old single African American female with four children spent 5 years of her life in and out of hospitals because of suicidal thoughts and behaviors. Initially, Sharon told her medical doctor she wanted to kill herself, and the doctor had her hospitalized, where she received a diagnosis of major depression. She was prescribed Prozac, and it was recommended that she receive individual and group therapy. Sharon was very upset about being hospitalized and insisted she would never kill herself because of her religious/spiritual convictions.

So it is not surprising that Sharon never took the prescribed medication, nor attended therapy sessions with regularity. Even when she did attend, she did not have a good experience, complaining that her therapist did not understand her.   It wasn't long before Sharon terminated therapy. When asked what she was planning to do about her illness, she stated, "*God will fix it.*" Throughout the five-year period, her children, ages, 15, 13, 12, and 11 were in and out of foster care because of their mother's illness.

Sharon was never able to keep a stable job, because it was too difficult for her to get out of the bed to go to work each day. Her home was a mess, and she lived in chaos. Sharon was in a love relationship, but her partner grew weary of Sharon's chaotic lifestyle, her negativistic view of the world, and her overall lack of motivation. This break-up made her even more depressed.

Sharon attended church regularly, and the church provided the only support system she had. Her relationship to God was very critical to her core beliefs, and she used prayer to help her to deal with problems. But she continued to be broken down and unable to function very well. It is important to pause here to say, that God can and will fix our brokenness, but sometimes He fixes it by sending the right people into our lives to help us.

Sharon had a very troubled childhood. Her mother abandoned her to follow her boyfriend to another state. Her grandmother (who was overwhelmed by 6 other grandchildren who also lived in the home) raised her. One of Sharon's uncles lived in the home for a long period of time, and he sexually molested her repeatedly from the time she was 5 until the age of 14. Consistent with the thinking of some young women who have been molested, Sharon believed the only way to attract a man was through her sexuality, and she was highly promiscuous. She had very low self-esteem, and guilt feelings persisted, especially about letting God down. It was difficult for Sharon to talk about her problems to anyone except God, because of trust issues.

Unfortunately, the case of Sharon is all too familiar because many of us are suffering, but fail to seek help from trained professionals. According to a national study by the *Black Women's Health Imperative* (2001), sixty percent (60%) of African American women in this country have symptoms of depression, but unfortunately, many of these women suffering from debilitating emotional problems fail to seek help from professional mental health providers. These findings speak to the need for African Americans to understand more about mental illness so they will feel more comfortable about reaching out for help.

In order for an individual to receive a clinical diagnosis of depression, he or she must experience a certain number of symptoms for a specific period of time, and the symptoms must interfere with the individual's daily functioning. In other words, if you are unable to go to work, maintain relationships, and you feel like giving up, you may be experiencing some form of depression.

There are different types of depression, such as Major Depression, Dysthymia, and Bipolar Disorder, each with different criteria. For example, in order to receive a diagnosis of Major Depression, the depressed mood must be present most of the day, almost everyday for a period of 2 weeks. While a diagnosis of Dysthymic Disorder is given when the depressed mood is present for more days than not for at least two years (DSM IV, 1994).

However, Bipolar Disorder is the most severe form of depression.

"People suffering from bipolar depression stay depressed longer, relapse more frequently, display more depressive

symptoms, show more severe symptoms, have more delusions and hallucinations, commit more suicides, require more hospitalizations, and experience more incapacitation. "

Coryell, Endicott, Andreason, & Keller (1985)

It is sometimes more difficult to distinguish bipolar from major depression because the symptoms are similar. However, bipolar depression tends to include extremely low energy, which explains why bipolar depressives prefer to stay in the bed. Dysthymic disorder tends to be the least consuming, because people suffering from dysthymia are more able to continue some level of normal functioning. However, these individuals tend to become chronic complainers, bringing others down with them, if they do not receive treatment (Maxmen & Ward, 1995).

Gender Differences in Depression

Men and women of all ethnic backgrounds suffer from depression; however, there are gender differences in the presentation of the disease. There is very little research available that tells us everything we need to know about the presentation of depression in the Black community, or the distinctive differences between Black men and women. However, there are a few reports that are worth noting:

1.   According to the 2000 *Minorities and Mental Health Report* of the U.S. Surgeon General, African American women tend to experience depression at a higher rate than African American men, and even though many of these women may not seek help for their problems, they are more likely to seek help than their male counterparts.

2.   African American females may face increased risk of

depression due to gender, poverty, perceived racism and discrimination, and other factors (Kohn & Hudson 2002).

3.   According to the *Black Mental Health Alliance*, 7% of African American men will develop depression during their lifetime, with a high percentage failing to receive treatment.

4.   According to the September, 2003 *Psychology Today Blues Buster Newslette*r, at least 6% of African American females have participated in some form of treatment for depression, but only 7% receive treatment as compared with 20% of the entire population.

It is important to note, however, that these findings may not be totally accurate because of the growing number of African American men and women who suffer without seeking help. Furthermore, many African Americans refuse to participate in research (for reasons that will be discussed in Chapter 4), so the findings must be interpreted with cau-tion.

The symptoms of depression also tend to be different for men and women of all ethnic backgrounds. For example, women suffering from depression are more likely to experience sadness, feelings of worthlessness, and excessive guilt, while men may become frustrated, discouraged, angry, irritable, and the risk of becoming violent. These findings are really important because there may be some correlation between African American males' depressed mood and violent behavior, especially since depression is sometimes characterized as anger turned inward.

In addition, African American men and women may avoid seek-ing help for different reasons. While it is clear that both groups tend to be uncomfortable with the stigma and negative stereotypes associated with mental illness; there are some pronounced differences between how African American men and women view mental illness.

African American men tend to view emotional problems as a sign of personal weakness; therefore, they avoid counseling and mental health services because they do not want to be viewed as weak. According to a report of the *National Mental Health Association*, 63% of African Americans believe that depression is a sign of personal weakness. Black men have been socialized to live by the motto: *"Be a strong Black man"* which implies total reliance on self for handling problems and situations. This thinking may also explain, in part, why churches may have such a hard time attracting and retaining Black men; and why some brothers have a difficult time connecting to the Spirit, which I believe is critical for optimal health and inner healing. There is no research to support this notion, however, John's case may shed some light on the subject.

I'm a Strong Black Man

John, a 56 year-old Black male was referred to me because of problems with anger and rage toward his employer. During our initial consultation, it was revealed that this troubled man had a very limited social support system, which was problematic because he clearly presented with symptoms of depression. While engaged in the intake process, John mentioned that he belonged to a church, but rarely attended. When I questioned his failure to attend church, he stated: *"I don't need to go to church. I can handle my own problems. My father taught*

*me in order to be a man, you have to handle your business, so that's
what I do."*

Sometimes depression in Black men goes untreated for the same
reason, it's not a manly thing to talk about your problems to outsiders.
However, Black men may be even more isolated, because many of them
do not share their problems or innermost thoughts and feelings with
anyone, including their spouses and partners.   Therefore, brothers may
have limited outlets for expressing their feelings, making them more at
risk of experiencing symptoms of depression.   Unfortunately, John was
not doing a very good job of handling his business, and if he had not
been mandated to receive treatment, his problems may have grown
worse.   It is important to note, that even though people are mandated to
receive treatment, they do not always benefit from those services.

Impact of Untreated Depression

When depression goes untreated, individuals are more at risk of
harming themselves, and in the case of some forms of depression, like
Bipolar Disorder, individuals may be at risk of harming others.
However, untreated depression also impacts daily functioning, the ability to set and reach goals, and the quality of one's relationships with others.   This was certainly true in the case of Jamie.

Your Sickness is Destroying Me

Jamie and Sarah had been married for 10 years and the quality
of their marital relationship was very poor. The couple got along well
the first few years of their marriage, but the quality of the relationship

had been going downhill for the past six years. The couple finally sought marriage counseling, and during one of the sessions Sarah reported Jamie's up and down mood, his irritability and anger, and his indifference toward her. This report raised a red flag, which prompted me to believe that Jamie might have been suffering from something other than marital discord.

After collecting the historical data, and conducting further assessment and evaluation, it was confirmed that Jamie was exhibiting symptoms of depression. Furthermore, it was possible that Jamie suffered from untreated depression most of his adult life, which may have explained, in part, why he had been married 3 times. Depression that is ignored can destroy a marital relationship, especially when couples are uneducated about the signs and symptoms of the disease.

Untreated depression also causes people to engage in destructive behaviors, such as overeating or under eating, illicit sexual behaviors, gambling, and reckless spending. Suffering people also self-medicate through the use and abuse of drugs and alcohol to numb them from the pain. In fact, some people suffering from depression are dually diagnosed with some form of substance abuse, which complicates treatment and the recovery process.

It is not easy for African Americans to admit they are hurting and in pain, so their depression continues to go untreated. However, repeated failure to acknowledge the pain will make it increasingly difficult for you or someone you love to lead a healthy and productive life.

As stated earlier in this chapter, African American men may suffer more because they tend to have fewer outlets for discussing their problems, while African American women may rely more heavily on the church, family members, and sistah friends for support. However, Black women may flock to sistahs who are unable to help them because they too may be struggling with the same issues. It is true that birds of a feather flock together. Therefore, it is highly important for broken people to confront their condition, and seek help from trained profes-sionals.

FOOD FOR THOUGHT

In this chapter, several situations have been presented to highlight what happens when we fail to acknowledge our pain, which is the first step toward inner healing. Perhaps it is time for you or a loved one to begin this process, especially if you are sick and tired of being broken. If you are sick and tired, this activity may be for you. It is not easy to confront self, and painful thoughts and memories may come up for you during the process. Therefore, after you have completed the activity, take time to meditate and pray. I do not believe that inner healing can be achieved without the love of God who provides comfort and peace during our time of greatest need.

Activity

1. What is bothering you?

    _____

    _____

    _____

2. Write down three ways that your state of brokenness
    has negatively impacted your life?

    _____

    _____

    _____

    _____

3. What do you want to do about it?

    _____

    _____

    _____

4. Other thoughts and reflections

    _____

    _____

    _____

    _____

MEDITATE ON THESE WORDS

Judge me, 0 God, and plead my case against an ungodly nation: 0 deliver me from the deceitful and unjust man; For thou art the God of my strength: Why does thou cast me off? Why go I mourning because of the oppression of the enemy? 0 send out thy light and thy truth: Let them lead me; let them bring me unto thy ho(v hill, and to thy tabernacles. Then will I go unto the altar of God, unto God my exceeding joy; yea, upon the harp will I praise thee, 0 God, my God: Why are thou cast down, 0 my soul? And why art thou disquieted within me? Hope in God: For I shall yet praise him, who is the health of my countenance, and my God

Psalms 43 - KJV

PRAY WITHOUT CEASING

Dear Lord, I am so tired of the pain. I know that I am not too broken to be fixed, so please give me the courage to admit how I am feeling to myself, so I can gain the necessary strength to admit how I am feeling to someone who can help me. Amen

CHAPTER TWO
I WILL SURVIVE

Trying to Overcome the Pain

"I don't care what I am going through, I will survive." This is a common statement in the Black community, and in some ways, this positive thinking has served us well. As a people, we are quite resilient and resourceful, with a built-in survival mechanism that works most of the time. Therefore, we have become skilled in using different survival strategies to help us to remain intact when we are close to losing our minds. But, we are not always successful. We sometimes use ineffective techniques for surviving the pain and suffering in our lives, but I would like to point out three we tend to use the most: (1) Keeping ourselves busy, (2) self-medicating, and (3) shopping. So let us first look at some of the ways we keep ourselves busy.

We keep busy by serving on too many committees, working too many hours, and spending too many nights in the week doing church work. Some of the Saints, especially sisters, are at the church every night of the week, because the church is a good hiding place. Unfortunately, keeping busy can contribute to new problems. I am afraid that if you were to follow some of us home, you might find chaotic living conditions, unruly children who perform poorly in school, and spouses who are on the verge of leaving because we are not home enough to participate in family life. Many of us find solace in God's house, doing the work of the ministry. But sometimes, we need more in order to survive, which was true in the case of Alice.

Seeking Solace in the Church

Alice arrived at the church at least 30-40 minutes late every Sunday, but she never missed. When she got there, she sat in the back of the church with her head hung low. She continued this pattern for the past six months, without fail. Alice is active in the ministry and she serves on four committees in the church. She is dressed modestly, and oh, she looks so sad; but somehow there is a ray of hope in her eyes, because she's in God's house.

Some of the church leaders wonder why Alice is always late for the services, because one of the rules for serving on committees in the church is to be on time for Sunday services. However, no one challenges her, because they know something is not right. They are right, because Alice suffers from severe depression. She like others in her situation believe if they can just make it to God's house, they will survive. For some, that belief may be valid, but for too many, additional help is needed.

Alice was going downhill fast, and it was becoming more and more difficult for her to crawl into the church each Sunday. Even though she stayed real busy doing church work, she continued to suffer without help, which was a huge risk to take when suffering from depression.

There are brothers who keep busy by working long hours everyday, and then spend their weekends participating in sports activities. There is nothing wrong with being active in the church or working overtime to increase one's financial base, but when one is keeping busy in order to mask pain, that is not a good thing.

In my work with clients, I have also found that hurting and broken people use busyness as a coping strategy. This strategy may work initially; however, when clinical depression sets in, it becomes increasingly difficult to keep going. People who substitute doing for being may ve even more stressed out when they are unable to perform. While some keep themselves busy, others self-medicate in order to survive the pain, which can contribute to additional pain and suffering.

What's Eating at Me?

Jessica is a 49 year-old female, who teaches 7th grade math and science. She has been married to Larry for the past 20 years, and she and her husband have had a difficult time in their marriage. The couple also lost a daughter 4 years ago, which has driven a greater wedge between them than ever before. Jessica teaches school everyday, serves on several boards, and serves in leadership in her church.

To the outside world, Jessica is the picture of health, wealth, and happiness. She is one who would be voted most likely to succeed, but she is sad on the inside. Jessica is usually away from home Monday through Thursday evenings, and her weekends are devoted to working at home, and attending church on Sunday. The entire cycle begins again on Monday.

Finally, on the advice of her physician, Jessica came to see me because her blood pressure was highly elevated, and the doctor suggested that she talk to a therapist along with managing her blood pressure through medication, diet modification, exercise, and rest. To this point, Jessica was not complying with those recommendations. She gained 50 pounds over a six-month period, and when asked about her eating habits, she stated, "*I eat just for the sake of eating. I do not even want to eat, but I just can't stop myself, even though I know it is killing me.*"

It has becoming increasingly apparent that eating has become a form of self-medicating, and a popular strategy for coping with internal conflict. This problem has become so significant in America, until diet programs are now shifting the focus away from what people are eating, to what's eating them. Jessica's energy level has significantly decreased, and even though she keeps going, fatigue has set in. Jessica remarked, "*I am so tired all the time, and I am finding it more and more difficult to keep going.*"

During the second session, Jessica revealed that their daughter died from complications of Leukemia, and it was discovered that Jessica blamed herself for her daughter's death; believing she could have done something to save her. Jessica was dealing with unresolved issues around her daughter's death. In addition, she and her husband were not there emotionally for each other because of the condition of their marriage. In fact, Jessica was upset with her husband because he was shut down during the process, which is not unusual for couples to experience marital problems after the death of a child because men and women sometimes handle grief differently.

For example, women are more able to express their pain, while men are sometimes less verbal, creating the illusion that they are not experiencing the same level of pain. While men may not visibly break down like women do, they tend to be torn up on the inside after the death of a child. Nonetheless, some women feel their husbands or partners are detached from the process. Unfortunately, Jessica and Larry have played the blame game with each other, making it more difficult for either of them to heal. So, Jessica eats to deal with the pain.

After a thorough assessment, it was apparent that Jessica was suffering from Dysthymia, a depressive disorder characterized by the following symptoms:

- *Poor appetite or overeating*
- *Insomnia or hypersomnia*
- *Low energy or fatigue*
- *Low self-esteem*
- *Poor concentration or difficulty making decisions*
- *Feelings of hopelessness*

It is very possible that Jessica's failure to deal with the loss of her daughter contributed to more serious depressive symptoms. However, through therapy, she has been able to get on the road to recovery and healing. She learned that self-medicating was not an effective survival strategy, rather, participating in individual therapy for her depression, marriage therapy to improve the quality of her marital relationship, and a grief and loss group have been much more effective strategies for achieving inner healing.

Jessica is now taking medication for hypertension and has developed a healthy eating and exercise regime. She walked around pretending that everything was going well by eating and ignoring the pain. However, during the course of therapy, she decided to pull the mask off, so the real Jessica could come forth and enjoy life.

Jessica helped us to see how we misuse food in order to feel better. Food has become a major stress reliever and anti-depressant in our community, and overeating tends to create new problems, such as obesity. Then obesity leads to other health challenges, such as hypertension, diabetes, and cancer.

Some of us think to ourselves: *If I can just find that candy bar, or go to Ben and Jerry's for my favorite ice cream, I'll feel better.* We may feel better for the moment, but it does not last very long. So eating may not be the best strategy for dealing with our brokenness. Do you have candy wrappers or other evidence of destructive eating habits hidden from public view? If so, that is a clear sign that you may be using food to numb the pain. You may be saying to yourself, *that's not my problem.* But perhaps, you can relate to the person who shops until they drop.

Living for the Mall

Marcia, a 30 year-old single Black female coped with her pain by staying in the mall. This young woman worked two jobs, and she had a hard time making ends meet. Yet, she shopped until she dropped. She had every toy and trinket one could have, but it was never enough. Nothing was good enough for Marcia, and her reckless spending created more problems for her. Marcia's car was repossessed twice, and she was forced to move three times because she could no longer pay the rent. If you saw Marcia, you would not believe she just wrote a bad check to buy an expensive dress for a black tie affair. She only wore name brand clothing and shoes, and she had so much stuff, until there was no more room in her closets. Not only would you find her at the mall during her lunch hour, after work, and on the weekend, you would also find her at the hair and nail salon. Remember, she had to look good. Girlfriend had it going on, or so it seemed; however, there was another side to her story.

Marcia's life was a wreck, and her excessive shopping was just a cover up for what was going on internally. Her parents divorced when she was 10 years old, and she lived with her mother with very little contact with her father. Marcia recalled experiencing feelings of sadness since adolescence, but she thought those were normal feelings so she silently removed them from sight. Marcia explained, *"I cried myself to sleep almost every night, because I thought no one cared."*

Marcia had an older sister who seemed to have it all, brains and beauty, and this sister was highly celebrated in the home. Therefore, Marcia began to view herself in a very negative light, and in an attempt to be acceptable to other people as well as to herself; she became obsessed with looking good and acquiring stuff and things. In order to look good, however, she had to shop, with or without adequate finances.

The more Marcia hurt on the inside, the more she felt compelled to buy a pretty dress or pair of shoes. *"Whenever, I felt that sadness come over me, I pulled myself up and headed for one of my favorite stores,"* stated Marcia.

Marcia started experiencing bad headaches, and even though she managed to shop, she felt a lack of motivation to do anything else. Her energy level dropped dramatically, and she had begun to run back and forth to see her medical doctor. After several tests were run, it was determined that Marcia was in good health, so her medical doctor referred her to a psychiatrist for a medication evaluation. Initially, Marcia refused to see the psychiatrist and tried other methods to help her deal with her problems. She was concerned about money since she depleted most of her financial resources in bad check charges. So Marcia began to take items back to the store to exchange them for other items. But no matter how much she went to the mall, she still was not getting any better.

The Marcia the public saw everyday was dressed immaculately from head to toe, but the Marcia nobody saw cried herself to sleep every night, and she was beginning to find it more and more difficult to get out of the bed in the morning. Finally, she broke. Unable to face the out-side world, Marcia decided to come out of hiding. She pulled out the referral her doctor had given to her and sought help for her brokenness. Marcia had suffered in silence for most of her life, and finally, the real Marcia was becoming free.

FOOD FOR THOUGHT

It is virtually impossible to adequately survive the painful effects of depression on your own, without getting the appropriate help. We saw that demonstrated in the cases of Alice, Jessica, and Marcia. We will remain broken unless we change some of the ineffective strategies we tend to use in order to overcome our pain. Remember, insanity is doing the same thing the same way, expecting a different result. Therefore, please take a few moments to participate in this activity, to propel you toward achieving inner healing.

Activity

1.   Write down three ineffective strategies you have used to over-
      come your pain.

      _____

      _____

      _____

      _____

2.   Why have these strategies been ineffective?

      _____

      _____

      _____

      _____

3.   What would you like to change about the way you have been
      doing things?

      _____

      _____

      _____

      _____

MEDITATE ON THESE WORDS

Preserve me, O God: For in thee do I put my trust, O my Soul, thou hast said unto the Lord, Thou art my Lord: my goodness extendeth not to thee; But to the saints that are in the earth, and to the excellent, in whom is all my delight. Their sorrows shall be multiplied that hasten after another god: their drink offerings of blood will I not offer, nor take up their names into my lips. The Lord is the portion of mine inheritance and of my cup: thou maintainest my lot. The lines are fallen unto me in pleasant places; yea, I have a goodly heritage. I will bless the Lord, who hath given me counsel: my reins also instruct me in the night seasons. I have set the Lord always before me: because he is at my right hand, I shall not be moved. Therefore my heart is glad, and my glory rejoiceth: my flesh also shall rest in hope. For thou wilt not leave my soul in hell; neither wilt thou suffer thine Holy One to see corruption. Thou wilt shew me the path of life: in thy presence is fullness of joy; at thy right hand there are pleasures forevermore.

Psalms 16: 1-11-KJV

PRAY WITHOUT CEASING

Dear Lord, I have been trying to deal with my brokenness in the only way I know how. I've been doing it my way, but my way is not working for me. Please help me to become more open to appropriate strategies for overcoming my pain. Amen.

CHAPTER THREE
GETTING TO THE ROOT OF THE MATTER

Common Explanations of Depression

"I don't know why I am feeling this way." Many people who suffer from depression do not know they are depressed, nor why they are depressed. There are many factors to explain why and how people become depressed, although researchers have not been able to pinpoint an exact cause. In this chapter, we will examine some of the common factors that contribute to the disease, taking into consideration specific variables that may make African Americans equally if not more at-risk of experiencing depression. According to the *National Institute of Mental Health*, people may become depressed because of one or more of the following factors: Biological factors, physical illness, personality traits, psychological issues, (e.g., faulty thinking), interpersonal problems, (e.g., divorce or family problems), and societal issues, (e.g., racism, sexism, and discrimination). It is beneficial for us to understand these factors in order to better insulate ourselves from the disease. I would like to include another factor: *Spiritual Disconnection,* because of the role that spirituality and religion play in the lives of African Americans.

Biological Causes of Depression

Depression tends to have a biological basis regardless of its root cause. Depression signals an imbalance in brain chemistry due to a deficiency in one of two neurochemicals (norepinephrine or serotonin) that is necessary for the proper functioning of the brain. If one lacks either of the two, severe depression will likely occur. This explains why medication can be helpful in alleviating some of the symptoms of depression. For example, if biologically untreated with antidepressants, bipolar depression typically persists six to nine months, with manic episodes lasting two to six weeks (Maxmen & Ward, 1995, p.219). However, depression may also be genetically linked and run in the fam-ily.

Generational Curse

Jane is a 53 year-old woman who suffers from Bipolar disorder. She has recurring thoughts of harming herself and has a long history of hospitalization with three prior suicide attempts. Jane's father also suffered from depression, and after years of battling the disease, he committed suicide when Jane was 23 years old. Jane's brother also committed suicide, and she believes her grandfather suffered from depres-sion as well.

It appears that depression runs in Jane's family, making them more predisposed to the disease than those whose family members do not suffer from depression. While everyone in that family may not suffer from the disease, some individuals suffer from depression even if it does not appear to be genetically linked. Therefore, one's genetic make-up alone does not account for depression, and there may be other fac-tors to take into consideration, such as major stressors, physical illness, and cognitive distortions.

Physical Explanations of Depression

It is also believed that people can become depressed in reaction to physical illnesses, such as stroke, cancer, diabetes, thyroid problems, and heart attack. Most debilitating diseases make people at risk of experiencing depressed mood at some point during their illness because they have a difficult time coping with major life changes that are inevitable when one becomes ill. But if the depression goes untreated, it can severely interfere with the individual's psychological and physical well being. The case of Michael illustrates the impact of physical illness on one's psychological and emotional well being.

The Mind-Body Connection

Michael is a 59 year-old African American male who is on dis-ability because he experienced a stroke. He led a very active life, and is now wheelchair bound because of paralysis on the left side. Initially, he was very hopeful about his prognosis, and believed he would regain the ability to walk and use his left side. However, after rigorous thera-py, he was still unable to use his left side and he became increasingly depressed, to the point of making statements like: *"I may as well be dead,"* and *"I'm such a burden on my family."*

Michael's wife described him as angry, and very difficult to get along with. She was worried that he would go over the deep end and take his own life because of his response to his physical condition. Michael did not have a history of depression prior to the stroke, nor was there evidence that any of his family members suffered from the disor-der. Therefore, it is possible that Michael's depressed mood was due to his physical ailment, and the inability to handle the stress and major life changes surrounding it. Since African American males tend to avoid seeking help for psychological problems, or even identifying their prob-lems as such, it was important for Michael to take the advice of his physician, who recommended that he seek help from a psychiatrist.

This issue is very important to consider in the African American community because we tend to suffer from certain health problems at a higher rate than other ethnic/racial groups, such as HIV-AIDS, breast cancer, prostate cancer, hypertension and diabetes. High poverty rates among some of our community members prevent us from getting the appropriate treatment for several health challenges, which may increase the likelihood that depressive disorders will persist. According to a recent report of *Black Health Care*:

- African Americans suffer with diabetes at three times the rate of Whites.

- African Americans experience heart disease at a rate of 40 per cent higher than that of Whites.

- Prostate cancer in our community is more than double that of Whites.

- HIV/AIDS is diagnosed more than 7 times that of Whites. In the past decade, deaths due to HIV/AIDS have increased dramatically in the African American community, and this disease is now one of the top five causes of death for African Americans.

•Breast cancer is higher for African American women than Whites, even though African Americans are more likely to receive mammograms.

Furthermore, depressive symptoms can occur in reaction to certain medications. So, it is critical for African Americans to have routine physical examinations and to visit the doctor when experiencing health challenges to prevent both physical and psychological problems from occurring. African Americans are just as unlikely to visit medical doctors for physical problems as they are psychological problems. Thus, in order to be healthy, **GET A COMPLETE CHECK-UP NOW**, especially when experiencing signs and symptoms of depression.

There are other physical factors that African American women must take into consideration when attempting to rule out depression. In addition to the normal mood swings that occur when women are pregnant; after the birth of a baby, women are at risk of experiencing postpartum depression, which tends to affect 1 out of 10 new mothers due to hormonal changes. Also, women suffering from PMS (Pre Menstrual Syndrome) and Menopause, are highly at risk of experiencing symptoms of depression due to hormonal imbalance.

I Can't Stand What I'm Feeling Inside

Janice a 48 year-old woman was experiencing hot flashes, vaginal dryness, and signs of anxiety and depression. She cried for no reason at all, and any little thing tended to upset her. Janice's husband of 20 years described her as moody and difficult to get along with, and their marriage was beginning to suffer severely. Janice was behaving like a different person, and her behavior was getting worse.

However, Janice began to realize that something was wrong, and after her husband announced that if things didn't change he was going to move out of the house, she decided to seek help from her primary care physician who referred her to a gynecologist. The doctor told her she was menopausal, and since Janice did not have a history of breast cancer in her family, she began hormone replacement therapy, and her depressive symptoms greatly improved.

Janice's situation underscores the need for African American women to consult with their physicians when they experience symptoms of depression, especially since women going through menopause may experience symptoms similar to those of depression. Not all women are able to participate in hormone replacement therapy, however, your doctor can advise you appropriately.

Personality Traits

All of us have personality traits, and researchers believe that certain traits may contribute to the onset of depression. Trait theorists believe that people are born with certain personality traits that are inherited, while others believe that personality traits are based on environmental forces (Plomin, 1994). However, there is growing agreement that personality traits are based on both genetic make-up and the environment in which one lives, works, studies, etc. On personality tests, individuals who score high on the following character traits (e.g., introversion, conscientiousness, dependent, and neuroticism) tend to be more at risk of being depressed:

1.   People who score high on the Introversion trait generally turn inward, and have little verbal and/or emotional exchange with the outside world.   These individuals may be more susceptible to depression.

2.   Conscientious personality types tend to have a high need for achievement, and they set high standards for themselves. This leaves them vulnerable if they are unable to reach the goals and expectations they have set, and ultimately depression can easily develop because of unmet goals and expectations.

3.   Dependent personality types are highly dependent on others for their self-esteem and sense of self-worth. These individuals may go from one bad relationship to another, because they have a difficult time being alone. These individuals tend to be very needy.

4.   Those who score high on the Neuroticism trait are prone to experience a high level of negative emotion and experience frequent episodes of psychological distress (Pervin & John, 2001).

I Need Thee Every Hour

Certain situations can trigger depression based on one's personality traits. For example, Jonathon is a highly dependent personality type. His wife recently divorced him after only three years of marriage, and he became severely depressed. His family and friends could not understand why he was experiencing such severe depression, when the woman he was married to did not treat him with dignity and respect. Jonathon became suicidal and had to be hospitalized. He was overly dependent on his wife for emotional support and self-esteem, and when she left him, he grew more and more hopeless and depressed. When individuals with personality traits that were listed above are bombarded with stressors, they tend to be more at risk of experiencing depression and other psychological distress.

There are a wide variety of personality theories that attempt to explain the cause of psychological disorders, such as depression, (e.g., psychodynamic, existential, humanistic theories); however, for the purpose of this book, we will focus on Cognitive Theory because of its comprehensive and well researched approach to treating depression.

Cognitive Explanations

Aaron Beck, a noted cognitive theorist, pioneered the cognitive approach to understanding and treating depression. The cognitive approach highlights the impact of the individual's thoughts, beliefs, images, perceptions, and other cognitive phenomena in the onset and duration of depression. While some cognitive theorists contend that faulty thinking and cognitive distortions occur because of depressed mood, Beck (1976) firmly held that an individual's thoughts about self, the world and experience, and the future, contributed to the onset of depression. Beck referred to these three components as the cognitive triad. However, other theorists contended that the cognitive triad was the consequence of depression. In other words, they suggested that depression negatively impacts one's thoughts about self, the world and experiences, and one's future. However, I tend to support Beck's view because of my experience in working with depressed clients.

As a Woman Thinketh, So is She

Beck contended that the way in which an individual appraises a situation is generally reflective of the individual's thoughts and visual images. Therefore, feelings of sadness are believed to be provoked by cognitive appraisals of situations, and/or thoughts about self, the world, and the future. This thinking is supported in the case of Mary, whose self-perceptions may have contributed to her brokenness.

Mary, a 20 year-old African American single female recalled feeling sad for a long time. Her mother died when she was two years old, and she never knew her father. Mary was raised by her maternal grandmother, but she was often teased by adult family members and told she didn't look like her mother or father. She never liked the way she looked, and always thought her siblings (two brothers and one sister) were much more attractive than she. In fact, she doubted whether she was even blood related to them.

Consequently, Mary had a very negative outlook on life, even during her school years. She was very introverted, and did not have many friends. Mary still does not have many friends, and she believes that she is ugly, unlovable, and not worth very much. She has become increasingly depressed which negatively impacted her life.

According to Beck's Cognitive Theory, Mary's broken condition is the result of the way she views herself and her perception of how others view her. Her sadness has been intensified because of faulty thinking and cognitive distortions. Mary believes she is inadequate and worthless, which has resulted in a hopeless future. She has allowed the voices from her past to perpetuate a self-fulfilling prophesy (confirming other's negative stereotypes and perceptions of you) which paralyzes and prevents her from living life to the fullest. Further, these negative attitudes have distorted Mary's perception of reality, which may have triggered depressive symptoms.

Our thoughts and self-perceptions can cripple us, and even make us sad. Some people in our community are not reaching their fullest potential because they are living out a self-fulfilling prophecy. We sometimes believe the internal voices that haunt us, and when opportunities arise for us to use our gifts and talents to further our careers, educational attainment, and future goals, we fail to rise to the occasion. Similarly, when we are confronted with our state of brokenness, we allow those same voices to stop us from seeking the help we are so badly in need of.

Interpersonal Relationships

"He just can't get along with anybody!" How often has this statement been made, signaling that the person has a difficult time with interpersonal relationships? Well, those of us who have difficulty maintaining good interpersonal relationships may be at risk of depressive symptoms. People may suffer from depression when a wide variety of interpersonal relationships (e.g., siblings, parent-child relationship, or friendship) go bad, especially marital relationships.

Situational and/or clinical depression is not uncommon after the break-up of a marriage. According to Keith and Norwood (1997), "*the psychological well-being of African Americans is enhanced by a satisfactory marriage, and threatened by a bad marriage.*" Therefore, couples who experience higher levels of marital strain may be at higher risk of experiencing symptoms of depression (Broman, 1993).

African American men and women face many challenges in their relationships, and personality and financial problems are slated to be major difficulties for couples to overcome. However, the fact that Black women are returning to school and seeking advanced degrees at higher rates than Black men, may contribute to some of the relationship challenges in the Black family. Black females' earning capacity has risen sharply over the past decade, increasing the likelihood of marital strain because of role reversal issues. Black women are sometimes in the position of bringing home the bacon, and cooking it too; which can compromise male-female relationships in our community. Such was the case for Wanda and Jim.

I Just Want to Advance Myself

Wanda and Jim had been married 30 years when he came home one night and announced he wanted a divorce. Wanda was devastated. This was her first love, the father of her three children, and she just couldn't believe this was happening to her. She thought these would be the best years of their lives, but they were not, especially after Wanda announced she wanted to go back to school.

She decided after her last child left home, that she wanted to pursue her education, so with only an AA degree, Wanda decided to go back to school to reach her goal of becoming a History teacher. After discussing her goals with her husband, he gave her the go ahead and was her chief supporter. However, once she finished her B .A. in education, she decided to pursue a doctorate in education to broaden her options. Her marriage began to go downhill. She thought all was well, but her husband began to complain that he was tired of cooking for himself, and eating alone while she was away at school.

In her attempt to pacify him, Wanda would cook several meals at a time and freeze them, so Jim would not have to cook. But that did not last long, because he was so accustomed to her cooking, cleaning, and taking care of everything, until he refused to settle for anything less. He was obviously having a difficult time with the reversal of roles. Things continued to go downhill, and divorce was imminent.

The thought of being alone and facing their family and friends, was more than Wanda could handle. She did everything she could to encourage him to change his mind, but Jim's mind was made up. He believed the marriage was over and that Wanda chose school and her educational advancement over their marriage. To complicate matters, Jim had a new love interest waiting in the wings.

Initially, Wanda experienced the normal depression that happens when one loses a loved one, but her condition began to worsen and she became very depressed and suicidal. She stopped eating and lost an enormous amount of weight. Wanda also began to follow Jim to see him and his new girlfriend together. Fortunately, her oldest daughter convinced her to seek psychological help for her depression, making it possible for Wanda to begin to heal from her brokenness. When we experience problems in important interpersonal relationships, it can take its toll on us psychologically.

Toxic love or family relationships can also contribute to depressed mood. Those of us that erroneously believe, **IF I JUST GET ME A MAN, THEN I'LL BE HAPPY,** are often highly vulnerable to getting sick. Some men and women believe that other people can make them happy, or erase their pain. Yes, people in our lives can contribute to our happiness, but no human being can totally heal our diseases. So even when we start out waiting patiently for Mr. or Ms. Right, we quickly open the door to allow Mr. or Ms. Wrong to walk in and take up res-idence.

I Gotta Have a Man

Danielle was 42 years old and she had never been married. She was feeling desperation about not having a husband or children. Her biological clock was ticking strong and loud. Danielle dated occasionally, but one night she decided to go out with her sistah friends, and while sitting in a nightclub, she met James, who she immediately began to call the *"man of her dreams."* As it turned out, James was more like the *"man of her nightmares."*

Danielle instantly became attached to this brother, and it wasn't long before she was announcing her engagement. Family and friends tried to warn her, especially when they noticed bruises on her arm, but she always defended him and told everyone to stay out of her business. Danielle married James six months after meeting him at the club, and after the honeymoon (that Danielle had to pay for because James lost all his money gambling), things began to go even further downhill. Danielle could no longer hide her bruises, and she admitted to her best friend that James was violent and abusive. Further, he was fired from his job, and Danielle had become the breadwinner for their family since that time.

Finally, Danielle fainted at work, and was taken to the local emergency room. She confided to the emergency room physician that she was being abused by her husband on a regular basis, and after a full physical examination, it was discovered that James had broken Danielle's arm during one of their altercations. After a lengthy discussion with her physician, Danielle decided to press charges, and James was arrested. During the course of her toxic interpersonal relationship with James, she became increasingly depressed until she received help for her brokenness.

During the course of therapy, it was not only important for Danielle to heal from her painful experience with James, it was also important for her to understand why she ignored all the warning signs alerting her that she was in a toxic relationship.

Societal Factors

People can sometimes suffer from depression because of events and situations that happen in one's environment, such as natural disasters (hurricanes, tornadoes, earthquakes, floods) and everyday social issues that invade our space, such as racism, discrimination, poverty, and family problems. However, I would like to focus on the latter, since social issues appear to exist with more regularity.

Due to a long history of racism, oppression, and discrimination, the African American community may be highly at risk of experiencing depression, as well as other psychological disorders, such as anxiety, post-traumatic stress disorder, and substance abuse disorders, at some point in their lifetime.

The Black community has probably suffered the most from the continual presence of racism and discrimination, beginning with the institution of slavery. Dr. Shelly Harrell has this to say about racism:

1.   *"It is a system of dominance, power, and privilege based on racial-group designations;*

2.   *It is rooted in the historical oppression of a group defined or perceived by dominant group members as inferior, deviant, or undesirable;*

3.   *It occurs in circumstances where members of the dominant group create or accept their societal privilege by: Maintaining structures, ideology, values, and behavior that have the intent or effect of leaving non-dominant group members relatively excluded from power, esteem status, and/or equal access to societal resources (Harrell, 2000)."*

Whether real or imagined, the impact of racism and discrimination on African Americans has the potential to produce mental health challenges and negatively impact self-esteem (Utsey, Ponterotto, Reynolds, & Cancelli, 2000; Williams & Williams-Morris, 2000; Utsey, 1998). We sometimes adopt the invisibility syndrome (a psychological experience where African Americans feel their personal identity and ability are undermined by racism) (Franklin, 1999; Parham, 1999; Wyatt, 1999, Yeh, 1999), making us even more vulnerable to psychological distress.

Further, race-related stress tends to be related to our mental health (Utsey, 1998), with racism being strongly related to psychological distress, including depression (Brown, Sellers, Brown, & Jackson, 1999).

Some believe that racism no longer exists, but nothing could be further from the truth. Racism is alive and well, but, it looks different, and it may have taken on a new form. I liken racism to the HIV/AIDS virus, because both keep changing forms, making both racism and AIDS very difficult to treat. Legal remedies are available, but lawsuits rarely change the mindset of a racist, or heal the wounds of innocent victims. In 1998, there were 7,755 hate crime incidents reported, with 67% of those incidents targeted toward African Americans.

Sadly, even some African Americans do not believe racism continues to persist, which may explain, in part, the sense of apathy that prevail in our community with regard to social justice and activism. Also, some of us have begun to identify with the oppressor, and we continue to demonstrate self-hatred by demonstrating hatred for each other because of the lightness or darkness of our skin.

Today, there is a new war on the horizon, the war between Black and Brown males. These two minority groups are fighting for the same piece of the pie, which has resulted in the senseless killing of Black and Brown men. This growing racial violence may be even more difficult to cope with.

We have learned how to insulate ourselves from the lethal effects of racism and other isms by developing healthy cultural paranoia, (a survival strategy used by African Americans). For example, when African American males avoid driving through certain neighborhoods at night, they are exhibiting healthy cultural paranoia because it has been proven that African American males experience racial profiling in certain communities. However, this strategy does not always protect us from experiencing symptoms of depression, and those who utilize unhealthy cultural paranoia (preoccupation with racism), are even more at risk of experiencing psychological distress.

Just Treat Me with Dignity and Respect

Our elders have been particularly impacted by the lethal effect of racism and discrimination, especially Black men. Mr. Williams, an 82 year-old veteran of the army was referred to me for psychological testing to determine his eligibility for veteran benefits. This well dressed senior man came into my office, and I noticed he had the saddest eyes I had ever seen. During the interview with Mr. Williams, he shared some of his experiences while in the military. In fact, he received an honorable discharge due to receiving a diagnosis of major depression.

Mr. Williams recounted the many racist incidents he experienced, and while talking his voice began to shake. I asked him if he wanted to take a break, he replied: '*I've needed to tell somebody about this for over 60 years, so I'll be all right*."

Mr. Williams proceeded to tell me about the overt racism that he experienced while in the military. Fellow soldiers, including his superiors, called him the "N" word, and other derogatory names on a regular basis. He wanted to do something about it, he wanted to fight back, but he felt powerless to do anything. *"I just sucked it all in. I would clench my fist in protest, because I knew if I said anything I would get into trouble. They didn't have to like me; I wanted them to treat me with dignity and respect."*

Eventually, Mr. Williams experienced a major trauma that probably sent him over the edge.

> *"I was stationed in Galveston Texas in 1943, when a race riot broke out in Beaumont Texas, because a Black man was accused of raping a White girl. Our camp was notified for help, but we were not allowed to go. All the black soldiers were left behind, while all the White soldiers were taken to Beaumont. They treated us like we were criminals, and took all the ammunition away from us and locked it up. We were left defenseless during a very trying time, and I just couldn't take it. I broke down, and when they took me to the infirmary, I was diagnosed with depression and given an honorable discharge."*

Mr. Williams fought back the tears as he continued.

> *"They sent me home with $250.00, and since I was never told to see a doctor when I returned home, I never received help. I did not have trust them to help me anyway. I have been struggling all these years, finding it difficult to keep a job, and having problems with my wife and kids. I just didn't know."*

Mr. Williams' story demonstrates how environmental factors, such as racism and discrimination can lead to depression. He was truly a victim, with limited educational and financial resources, and his experiences in the military have made it very difficult for him to lead a productive life. Many of us have also been exposed to racist and sexist treatment on the job, and we tend to ignore it, making us more vulnerable to mental illnesses, such as depression.

Will I ever be good enough?

Lisa, a 40 year-old university professor recently sought psychological services because of terrible headaches and insomnia that had no apparent physiological basis. During our time together she revealed that she received a teaching fellowship that was given to people of color in order to increase the number of faculty of color. Lisa shared her story that is experienced too often in communities of color.

*"I was never accepted. Some of my white colleagues treated
me as though I didn't belong there. Even though I worked
harder than any of the faculty in my department, and
accomplished more than they did, I was still the odd woman
out. I never thought it bothered me until I came up for
promotion. I was basically told that I did not deserve to be
promoted so soon. Now that I think about it, that is when my
feelings of sadness really became pronounced. It wasn't until I
was sitting on an airplane in route to Atlanta, Georgia that I
began to cry uncontrollably on the plane. I had never done
this before. I had always been able to control my emotions,*

*but the more the passenger next to me attempted to console
and comfort me, the more I cried. I finally realized that I was
badly broken and bruised, and I needed help. They still think
we are inferior to them."*

So many African American men and women work on jobs
where they are constantly verbally or silently challenged about their
credentials or qualifications. After a while, we begin to doubt our
own competence. These environmental factors become fertile ground
for depression and other mental illnesses. Also we are prone to
work ourselves into the ground to prove that we are competent, and
good enough to be there, which can negatively impact both our mental
and physical health.

Additionally, African Americans can experience acculturative
stress (stress that occurs because minorities are not allowed to
successfully acculturate into the dominant culture). Some of us
continually attempt to modify our beliefs and values in order to be
accepted into the dominant culture, even though our beliefs and values
may be incompatible.

We also find it difficult to affirm ourselves, and fail to embrace
our own ethnic/racial identity because of our over reliance on the
dominant culture for affirmation that may be inauthentic or it just may
never happen. This identity confusion contributes to brokenness and
inner turmoil. Further, it is difficult to admit to ourselves that we
need to be affirmed by the dominant culture.

That's Just the Way Men Are

Black women are especially vulnerable to sexism, and sexual harassment, which may also contribute to their psychological well-being. Some women tend to down play sexist behavior and sexual advances by explaining men's bad behavior as follows: **THAT'S JUST THE WAY MEN ARE**.

During the Anita Hill and Clarence Thomas hearings, it was fascinating to hear some Black women's opinions. There were those who believed Judge Thomas was guilty of sexual harassment, and took advantage of this young, unsuspecting hard working Black female. However, other Black women thought the whole thing was stupid. I vividly recall one sistah's remarks: *"Anita is just mad because he got with a white woman. She knows we go to work hoping a fine brother will hit on us."*

Well, I am going to reserve my opinion about the Anita Hill/Clarence Thomas controversy for now. However, I am afraid that some Black women may have been socialized to normalize inappropriate sexual advances and sexism in general, making them more vulnerable to internalized rage and sadness because they really do not like what is happening to them.

Our community has also been hard hit by other social issues that may be contributing to the onset of depression in the lives of our people, such as poverty. While we have certainly made great strides in terms of a growing middle to upper class segment of our population, the poor are still with us. When a community is lacking in financial resources, and individuals do not have their basic needs met, such as housing, food, clothing, transportation, and childcare, that community is much more at risk of experiencing psychological distress. According to Culbertson (1997):

> ***"Poverty is a statistically powerful risk factor for the onset of depression."***

As stated earlier, poverty may contribute to psychological distress, especially among Black women. The *U.S. Census Bureau* in 2003, (which I cite with caution), issued the following report regarding the financial status of African Americans in the United States:

•The median annual income (which means the average) of African American households is $29,470, which is just under the all-time high reached in 2000, with an annual per capita income for African Americans of $14,953.00, which is unchanged from 2000, after adjusting for inflation.

•8.1 million of the 34.7 million African American population is classified as poor.

•When comparing poverty rates to other groups, Asians represent 9.2%, Whites 11.4%, Hispanics 23.6%, and African Americans 27.3%, which suggests that African Americans with and without children under the age of 18 have the highest poverty rate of all the other major groups.

•African Americans also represent the lowest median income. The Median Income for Blacks in 1967-2001 was 19,000 – 29,470, as compared to   Hispanics from 1973-2001 of 29,000 – 33,565, Whites

33,000 -- 45,000 and Asians, who represent the highest median income of 48,000 – 53,635.

•According to National statistics, African Americans represent the largest homeless population 45% as compared to 32% White, 4% Hispanic, and 3% Asian.

It is true that the poor will be with us always, but sadly, this reality suggests that mental and physical illnesses will also be with us.

Another important environmental factor to consider in understanding the causation of depression in the Black community may be the family environment. The family was the most significant tradition for health and healing in our community. Back in the 80's there were five strengths that helped to promote survival, advancement, and stability in the African American community (Bass, Acosta, and Evans, 1982):

Strong kinship bonds
Strong work orientation
Adaptability of family roles
Strong achievement orientation
Strong religious orientation

However, poverty, drug and alcohol abuse, and divorce and separation have seriously affected these strengths, making the community at risk of experiencing more severe stressors than ever before, which can ultimately lead to depression. Our family structure has changed over the past 20-30 years, and the most recent *U.S. Census Bureau* reports the following statistics:

1.   Of the 11.8 million African American children recorded at the time of this census taking, 41% of them live in homes maintained by their mothers, 34% live in homes with both parents, and 13% live in a grandparent's home.   Therefore, at least 54% of African American children do not have a father in the home.

2.   Close to 45% of Black children are in public foster care, with another 40% representing juveniles in legal custody.

Many African American women are broken down because they are raising children alone, with little to no financial support from their *"baby's daddy."* These mothers are at high risk of experiencing symptoms of depression. The environmental stress of trying to raise a boy to be a man, and to keep him out of the gang and alive, is very pronounced in the Black community, and it can be very draining. Women work tirelessly to raise sons to be men, but many of them become a man "just like mama," since women do not know what it is like to be a man, nor do they understand some of the issues that are specific to men. Many Black mothers have successfully raised young men to be responsible and productive citizens. However, young men who are raised without fathers or other positive male role models may not learn everything they need to know in order to maximize their manhood (Kunjufu, 1990).

We have long been under the erroneous assumption that only boys need their fathers, but we are finally beginning to understand that girls need their dads too!   Loving fathers foster a sense of self-esteem and self-worth in young girls, which makes them less vulnerable to victimization by boys and men who seem to prey on the innocent.   Many young ladies in our community are looking for a dad in all the wrong places, as they begin the search to find a "daddy replacement." In addition, some young girls seek out older men to fill this void. This is tragic, because some of these young ladies end up with more than they bargained for, such as pregnancy, sexually transmitted diseases, or worse, abuse and violence, all leading to sadness and despair.

Mothers and fathers who are raising children alone often become angry, even if their ex's are involved in the lives of their children, which contributes to increased hurt and anger in these children. Custodial parents who are unable to forgive their ex's for leaving (even when they financially support the children), usually talk negatively about their ex's, making it more difficult for children to love and embrace both parents. When custodial parents fail to give children permission to love both parents equally, children experience increased psychological damage that is carried over into adulthood. Further, when the non-custodial parent constantly criticizes and talks negatively about the custodial parent in front of the children, the same damage is done.

I Need my Dad

Raven's parents divorced when she was 8 years old. She and her father had a strong relationship from the time she was born, but when her parents divorced, everything changed. Her mother was very angry with Raven's dad, and she heard her mother express anger toward dad on a regular basis. Raven's mother talked negatively about her father to family, friends, and anyone who would listen, and sadly these conversations were spoken in Raven's presence. It wasn't long before

Raven felt she had to choose sides, and she chose her mother since she lived with her. Furthermore, the mother played the victim role, which placed Raven right smack dab in the middle of the drama between her mother and father.

It us difficult for our children to understand that both parents contribute to the demise of the marital relationship when one parent has more influence than the other parent. Today, the situation has not gotten much better, and even though Raven is 25 years old, she continues to suffer psychologically because of the loss of her dad. He did not die, but he may as well have died, because he was not allowed to be active in her life.

Raven was referred to me because she was suffering from symptoms of depression, such as agitation and irritability, lack of motivation and energy, depressed mood, and over eating. In her teen years, Raven began to look for a *"daddy substitute,"* but she always became involved with the wrong guys. Raven was crying out, **I NEED MY DAD,** but her family environment was not very supportive of her need to be in relationship with both parents.

I sincerely hope that parents will take heed to Raven's story, because the environment you create for them will either help them to thrive or help to destroy them.

A toxic home environment where physical violence and emotional abuse prevail can also lead to depressed mood. Domestic violence is felt in the Black community, and it not only negatively impacts the two sparring partners, but the children who are forced to live in that environment usually suffer more. Women are not the only victims of domestic violence, for men also experience abuse. However, many men suffer in silence about the abuse because they are too ashamed to admit a female abused them.

I am a columnist for a local newspaper, Inland Valley News in Pomona, California, where I respond to questions from the public relat-ing to relationship and mental health issues. Domestic violence is such an important issue in the Black community, until I think it is important for me to share my response to a recent question that was posed to me. Perhaps you or someone you know and love may be able to benefit from it.

I'm Getting Tired of the Violence

Everybody keeps telling me that I should leave my husband of 10 years because I have made the mistake of telling my friends and family every time he has pushed me around. I know I should keep our business in the home, but sometimes it gets really hard to do that. One of my friends even said the words "domestic violence" to suggest that my husband is getting physical with me. He is not violent, he is just under a lot of pressure, and when I emotionally push him to the limit, he phys-ically pushes me or says mean things to me. I realize I deserve it, and when it's over, he is the most wonderful man in the world. I have noticed, however, the pushing occurs more frequently, and I am begin-ning to become more afraid that he will really lose his temper. After all, he is under a lot of pressure. I would like to ask you, is my hus-band abusing me? If so, what can I do about it?

Get Some Help for You

I think you already know the answer to your own question. You and your husband may be fully engaged in the cycle of abuse. According to the 1998 Commonwealth Fund Survey, close to 1/3 of all American women report being physically or sexually abused by a boyfriend or husband during their lifetime. Furthermore, the National Domestic Violence Hotline reported in December of 2001, that   more than 700,000 calls for help were received. This is an indication that domestic violence must be taken seriously.

Many women like you, are in a state of denial, and sometimes the violence is taken seriously too late. Both men and women are vic-timized by domestic violence, however, 92% of all domestic violence crimes are committed by men against women. There are three forms of abuse: Physical, emotional, and sexual abuse. Emotional abuse can be equally harmful as physical and sexual abuse. All forms of abuse are based on power and control.

According to Nikki Katz:

"An abusing partner blames you for mistakes, prevents you from seeing family or friends, curses you, humiliates you, mocks you or says mean things, forces you to have sex or forces you to engage in sex that makes you feel uncomfortable, restrains, hits, punches, slaps, bites or kicks you, intimidates or threatens you, even prevents you from leaving

the house, getting a job, or continuing your education, destroys personal property, behaves in an overprotective way or becomes extremely
jealous, or threatens to hurt you, your children, pets, family members,
friends, or him or herself."

He or she only has to do one of the items mentioned above for
the relationship to be considered abusive. It is not unusual for battered
women to forgive their spouses and partners, because the batterer
becomes the loving spouse his wife or partner has always wanted him
to be. So get your head out of the sand, admit what is really going on,
and get help for yourself. Please know, **YOU DO NOT DESERVE TO
BE ABUSED.** You could benefit from counseling, and your spouse
could benefit from an anger management program, but he needs to ini-
tiate the latter process. Remember, you deserve to be in a loving and
nurturing environment, and it's up to you to make that happen. If you
continue to deny the existence of violence in your home, you may
become one of the statistics who does not survive the abuse. Abused and
abusive men and women are usually sad people in desperate need of
help.

> **If you are a victim of domestic violence, please
> contact the 24 hour National Domestic
> Violence Hotline (800) 799-7233 or the Rape,
> Abuse, Incest National Network,
> (800) 656-HOPE.**

Spiritual Disconnection

Some believe that African Americans who are not connected to the Spirit of God are at risk of experiencing psychological distress. We have enjoyed a long tradition of being spiritually connected to God, and that connection is credited for serving as a major buffer for our ancestors against the institution of slavery, and all the other societal infractions perpetrated against our people. Regardless to our wide variety of religious persuasions, our faith and hope in God have sustained us during some of the most traumatic events and situations. Our faith is exercised and celebrated by assembling ourselves together to worship our God.

Therefore, spirituality and religion play a major role in the lives of our people, and when we become disconnected from our spiritual source, it is not surprising that we become depressed or suffer from other psychological disorders. According to Dr. Carlyle Fielding Stewart, III:

"To be 'spiritual' from an African American perspective, is to live wholly from the divine soul center of human existence. This center is the core of the universe and the quintessential impetus driving the quest for human fulfillment. Thus, African American spirituality connotes the possession of a soul force spirit that divinely mediates, informs, and transforms a human being's capacity to create, center, adapt, and transcend the realities of human existence."

Through the spiritual connection, Black folk can be liberated from the fangs of racism, oppression, and discrimination, with the possibility of transcending to a higher plane, when forced to deal with the oppressor on a daily basis. Therefore, our connection to the spirit may be essential for optimal health and well being.

While the research on this topic is inconclusive, spirituality and religious involvement are still believed to play a powerful role in the lives of African Americans. African Americans who are connected to the Spirit tend to have greater overall life satisfaction; are more insulated from mental illnesses, such as depression; and are physically healthier with reduced mortality risk among the elderly.

Spirituality and healthy religiosity provide opportunities for connection to important social resources and support, the creation of positive self-perceptions, and the promotion of life styles that minimize the risk of debilitating stressors. *"Religious practices, rituals, and beliefs may provide specific coping resources for African Americans* (Ellison, 1998)."

Trouble Won't Last Always

Valerie, a 75 year old woman living in an assisted living home was referred to me because of depressive symptoms. During the intake process, I learned that this elder experienced enormous trauma in her life, but her relationship with God enabled her to cope. Valerie was married to the love of her life, and four short years after their wedding, he was tragically killed in a senseless shooting accident, leaving her with a set of twins to raise alone. Valerie never remarried, and devoted her entire life to her two daughters. Sadly, death struck again, and both of her girls were killed while riding together to a family function.

While discussing the deaths of her loved ones, Valerie stated:

"I usually do okay, but this is the 10th year anniversary of their deaths, and I'm feeling pretty bad right now, but trouble won't last always." When I asked Valerie how she coped with all the losses, she replied: *"I turn it all over to God. I pray in season and out of season. Sometimes I get a little weak and heavy, but that does not last too long. I just pray and sing my old songs, and I know everything is going to be all right. I'm all right with Jesus and He's all right with me."*

It did not take me too long to discover that Valerie's ability to use religious practices and rituals, such as prayer, and singing spiritual songs had been valuable coping resources during her lifetime, and without that spiritual connection, she may not have been able to survive. Spiritual development is essential to human development (Queener & Martin, 2001).

Why am I disconnected?

There are several reasons some African Americans may be spiritually disconnected. First, some of us may not have sufficient time to nurture our relationship with God. The quest to be wealthy and popular may supercede our need for prayer, meditation, and daily devotion, leaving us spiritually bankrupt.

Second, Black folk are also disconnected from the spirit because of our inability to forgive and let go. Many people suffering from depression are unable to forgive those who have hurt them, creating a prison for themselves instead of a prison for the person who hurt them. Frederick Buechner says it this way:

"Of the Seven Deadly Sins, anger is possibly the most fun. To lick your wounds, to smack your lips, over grievances long past, to roll over your tongue the prospect of bitter confrontations still to come, to savor to the last toothsome morsel both the pain you are given and the pain you are giving back, in many ways it is a feast fit for a king. The chief drawback is that what you are wolfing down is yourself. The skeleton at the feast is you."

Third, others are disconnected from the spirit because people, situations, and traditions in the church have hurt them, (e.g., the pastor failed to visit them when they were ill, they were not recognized for their hard work, or they were not allowed to lead a song in the choir). I am sure these situations can be harmful, but perhaps the church leaders were not trying to hurt you intentionally. But sometimes, the church can do harm to its sheep, especially if the sheep are already broken, contributing to a broken spirit. That is exactly what happened in the cases of Candy and Rhonda.

Don't come up in here like that!

Candy, a young 23 year old African American female began therapy, and one of her therapeutic goals was to become reconnected to the spirit of God and to become active in her church again. In order to help her reach the goal she set for herself, it was important for me to understand how she became disconnected, so she shared her heart breaking story with me.

"I was new to the faith. My parents never went to church, and didn't know very much about God, but I did know that I needed something. My life was a wreck. I hung out with bad boys, and I had gotten into some pretty bad situations. But one day, I met a lady at the store who invited me to her church. I was very hesitant at first, but I knew something had to change in my life, so I decided to take her up on her offer and I went to church. I really liked the church, so I began to attend pretty regularly. I even got saved and was planning on getting baptized. I was so excited until I wanted everyone in my family to experience what I was experiencing. They were not interested in coming, but it was my plan to get them all there when I got baptized. The church wasn't too large, but people dressed pretty nice. They wore their 'Sunday Clothes' while I wore my street clothes, because that was all I had. I didn't care, because I was getting something I really needed, and a few of the people were really nice to me, so I thought my attire was acceptable. Boy was I wrong! One Sunday morning I arrived at church a little late and the usher stopped me because the Scripture was being read. While standing at the door, she leaned over and told me I looked like a streetwalker, and she even went so far as to say, 'Don't come up in here like that again.' I was really taken back by her comments, but more than anything, I was hurt and devastated. The God they were teaching me about was loving and kind, but that was not my experience with the woman at the door.

So I followed her instructions, and I never went back to that church again."

He or She who is without Sin Please Cast the First Stone

Rhonda grew up in the church. She has been a lead singer in the choir from the time she was 16 years old until last year when she turned 40. Rhonda had been dating a married man for the past 10 years. No one in the church knew she was involved in this relationship until one year ago, and when the pastor's wife found out, it was brought to the attention of the pastor. The pastor counseled with Rhonda, and she made the commitment to end the relationship. She asked the pastor and his wife to forgive her, and she asked God for forgiveness, so she felt a sense of relief from the burden of guilt.

Rhonda had been a member of this church since childhood, so she trusted the pastor and his wife to not expose her publicly. However, when she went to church the following Sunday, the pastor used her situation as the theme of his sermon, featuring Zezebel as the leading character. Her name was called out and Rhonda was asked to come to the altar to be cleansed of her sins, and right there in front of church members and visitors, she was asked to resign from the choir. Rhonda was devastated, and she stated to me:

"I just could not believe what the pastor did to me, especially since we spoke in confidence. I came to him and his wife and admitted that I was wrong, even though the man I was seeing was not living with his wife when we got together. They are

legally married, but separated. I personally know of others in the church who are committing sin, but they all judged me harshly. They must have forgotten what the Bible says: 'Let he who is without sin cast the first stone.' That was a sad day for me, and when I left church that day, I never stepped foot into another church. Ever since that day, I have not been the same. God and my church were everything to me, and now I feel like a fish out of water."

Sometimes the church is the only army that shoots its wounded. Hurting people, regardless to whether they have made mistakes or not, can easily be hurt by other hurting people in the church, resulting in spiritual disconnection. These hurting people fail to realize that the church is made up of hurting and broken people who are prone to do and say things that are hurtful and harmful. We must constantly remember the church is a hospital with sick and hurting people, so we must demonstrate love and kindness at all cost.

The African American church is not only a religious institution; it is also a social and political institution. Many of us find our sense of purpose and validation through the church. Therefore, those who are disconnected from it, for whatever reason, are more prone to suffer psychologically. In the cases of Candy and Rhonda, they both experienced psychological distress because of that disconnection.

I do not want to paint a bleak picture of the Black church, because I do believe in the inherent value of the church to our people. But I think these examples are important to help us to understand some of the factors that contribute to depression and other psychological disorders in our community. Furthermore, I am hopeful these situations will help the church community to better understand its role in contributing to the psychological well being or demise of its parishioners.

Fourth, we may feel disconnected because of guilt feelings associated with sin and/or mistakes of the past. Some of us have a difficult time forgiving ourselves for the sins we commit, so we may live in a state of guilt and self-punishment, especially when we do not believe we will be redeemed. Therefore, we find ourselves disconnected from our spiritual source because we believe we have disappointed God. That is exactly how Jackie felt, making her at risk of psychological and physi-cal distress.

God, I'm Sorry I let you Down

Jackie, a 23 year-old college student in her senior year became pregnant. She was in a committed relationship with the young man, but she decided to have an abortion against everybody's wishes because they were not prepared to care for a child. Jackie was a youth leader in the church she grew up in, and she was very active, so this was not an easy decision for her to make. She began to become depressed before actually having the abortion because of her strong religious beliefs and values, but she did it anyway. After the abortion, Jackie began to change. This once bubbly and outgoing young lady was now becoming withdrawn, and her friends noticed she did not want to go out with them anymore. It was also difficult for her to go to her church, and she resigned her position with the youth group.

Jackie's mother was finally able to get her to seek counseling, and during our sessions Jackie discussed the enormous guilt feelings she was experiencing, making her more and more depressed. Jackie believed she had let God down, and she did not know how to reconnect with Him. Many Christians struggle with abortion and other controversial issues, and continue to be broken because of them.

Without a loving family and church family to offer redemption and solace, these individuals may allow the guilt to weigh them down too heavily. Black women in the church have had abortions and committed other sins as we all do, but they seem to have forgotten the pain associated with that decision. Too many of us parade around with a *mask of perfection* on, when people (a child, spouse, friend) in our experience really need us to be real about our own limitations so they will not judge themselves so harshly.

I am reminded of a story I once heard, where a young adult com-mitted suicide. In the suicide note she wrote to her father, she explained that she had no choice but to take her life because her father was perfect and expected her to be perfect; and she realized she could never meet his expectations. The father threw himself down to his knees in shame and despair, and began to cry because he realized he failed to share his personal failures and shortcomings with his daughter.

Unfortunately, this father will always wonder if he had been open enough to self-disclose, would his daughter still be alive. Perhaps had he taken off his *mask of perfection*, his daughter may not have felt she was all alone in her struggle.

Healthy church folk must become more transparent,
because the life you save may be someone you love!

Finally, we are sometimes disconnected because we are angry with God. When we experience the death of a loved one, unfair treatment on the job, family problems, failure to find Ms. or Mr. Right, or what we perceive to be broken promises by God, we get mad at Him, and shortly thereafter we disconnect from the Spirit. We sing the lyrics, *"He may not come when you want Him, but He'll be there right on time,"* yet when He fails to come to our rescue when we call Him, or when he disappoints us, it's over for God. Once again, being disconnected from the Spirit may contribute to a broken spirit.

It is important to note, that all case examples and situations in this section of the book are based on the Christian understanding of the Spirit in order to accurately support the points that are made by the stories that have been shared. I fully acknowledge and respect other views, but since I am a Christian, and the majority of my clients come from a Christian background, it is important that I speak from the perspective I know best.

FOOD FOR THOUGHT

We have reviewed several explanations for the occurrence of depression. However, the current research is clear that depression can best be explained by the combination of some of the factors mentioned in this chapter. The question for you is; what has caused you to be broken? Did a close family member have the disease and pass it onto you?

Or did life's situations and/or your appraisal of those situations cause you to be sad? What about your disconnection from God; has that made you sad?

Some of my colleagues may differ with me on this point, but I believe it is important to understand the origin of the disease, as well as some of the triggers, so that you will be able to fight the disease more efficiently. Furthermore, if your depression is the result of one or more of these variables: faulty thinking (sometimes referred to as stinking thinking), bad interpersonal relationships, or environmental stressors, understanding the root cause may be a critical part of the healing process. Therefore, let's continue on our journey toward inner healing and wholeness, by participating in this short activity. Please do not forget to meditate and pray today.

Activity

After reading about the various causes of depression, which one makes the most sense to you and why?

_____

_____

_____

_____

_____

_____

_____

MEDITATE ON THESE WORDS

When you pass through the waters, I will be with you; and when you pass through the rivers, they will not sweep over you. When you walk through the fire, you will not be burned; the flames will not set you ablaze, " says the Lord

Isaiah 43:2 KJV

PRAY WITHOUT CEASING

Dear Lord, I have learned more about my brokenness, and I ask that you continue to guide me through the rough waters ahead, as I seek inner healing. Amen

CHAPTER FOUR
THEY JUST DON'T UNDERSTAND ME

Identifying and Removing Cultural Barriers to Treatment

"*I know I need help, but they just don't understand me,*" stated a new client who was suffering from depression. This 32 year-old man was diagnosed with major depression when he was 28 years old, but he could not seem to find a therapist that could understand his unique perspective and worldview. He did have one therapist he felt comfortable with, but he was an intern who would only be at the clinic for a short time. This problem speaks to the issue of cultural competence, which is a necessary component for mental health providers to possess when treating African Americans and other people of color.

What is Cultural Competence?

According to Cross, Bazron, Dennis, Issacs, and Benjamin (1989), "*Basic cultural competence, accepts and respects cultural differences; is committed to promoting cultural knowledge, self-evalua-*

tion, and acknowledgment of the dynamics of difference; and adapts services to fit the cultural population they serve."

What does it mean to provide culturally competent care?

"Culturally competent mental health care relies on historical experiences of prejudice, discrimination, racism, and other culture-specific beliefs about health or illness, and culturally unique symptoms and interventions with each cultural group to inform treatment. " (Dana, Gehn, & Gonwa, 1992)

African Americans have not always received culturally competent care, making it more difficult for them to seek help from mental health professionals, or to continue treatment. This is problematic since many of our people are in need of these services. For example, a young woman suffering from depressed mood found a therapist through her insurance company. The therapist was European American, and when the young woman told the therapist she was having marital problems, the therapist suggested that she separate from her husband. Keep in mind, the woman's husband of ten years was not abusive, and the couple had strong spiritual beliefs that prevented them from contemplating separation and/or divorce. The couple were livid with the therapist, and even though the wife was suffering from depression, she terminated treatment.

In this chapter, we will identify some of the major cultural barriers that may hinder African Americans from reaching out for help, such as the Black church, cultural mistrust, stigmatization, misdiagnosis and medication, discomfort and unfamiliarity with traditional interventions and strategies, identity/acculturation issues, conflicting world-views, and poverty. Furthermore, we will also look at the cultural barriers that mental health providers must work to remove in order to provide effective services to this unique population.

Hopefully, this chapter will help those in need of psychological help to overcome and remove some of the cultural barriers in order to experience inner healing. In addition, I am hopeful that mental health professionals will find this chapter useful in fostering an understanding of the cultural world of African Americans; as well as to confront and challenge their own negative perceptions, stereotypes, and myths that limit the effectiveness of services to African Americans.

Barriers from Clients' Perspective

Barrier #1: The Black Church

The Black church is considered to be a vitally important institution in its community. I believe the church has the potential to be extremely effective in meeting our diverse needs. However, the church can also serve as a significant barrier if church leadership devalues the role of professional psychology and counseling, and does not encourage its people to seek help from mental health professionals when their problems are clearly outside the scope and practice of the pastor and other church leaders.

Pastors have increasingly approached me to come and speak at their churches about mental health, and they have referred clients whose issues were outside their scope of practice. Without that kind of collaboration and support, I believe many African American church folk would continue to ignore their pain and suffer in silence. Therefore, it is important for the church community to become more knowledgeable about mental illness to help remove the stigma prevents the people of God from seeking help outside the church.

Barrier #2: Cultural Mistrust

Many Black people do not trust the current mental health system any more than systems in the past, creating another powerful barrier to seeking help, cultural mistrust. Black folk may not seek help for mental health problems because they do not trust a system that has a long history of being racist, oppressive, and discriminatory since the African Maafa (a term developed by Marimba Ani (1994) to refer to The Great Disaster, when the forced dislocation of millions of Africans from their families, communities, and cultural heritage occurred, leading to the legacy of slavery). Other atrocities, such as racial classification and designations, IQ testing, sterilization laws, and racial experimentations all contributed to African American's distrust of the systems and institutions that have traditionally oppressed them.

Not only are African Americans apprehensive about seeking help from these institutions, we are apprehensive about participating in research studies of all types. This is unfortunate because without research studies, very little is known and understood about African Americans' attitudes, beliefs, feelings, and practices. Furthermore, empirical studies are sometimes necessary to back up claims about what constitutes best practices for treating African American clients.

There were many events and situations that impacted Blacks' attitudes toward mental health and psychology, however, one of the most horrific events in U.S. history was the Tuskegee Syphilis Experiment (Roy, 1995). This event was another tragic expression of America's inhumanity toward African Americans.

Between 1932 and 1972, the U.S. Public Health Service (PHS) conducted experiments on 399 African American males who were primarily illiterate sharecroppers from one of the poorest counties in Alabama. These unsuspecting men were told they were being treated for bad blood when in actuality they were in the late stages of syphilis. There was never any intention on the part of the U.S. Health Department to provide treatment for the Syphilis, because the actual data for the experiment were to be collected from the autopsies of these men after their deaths. They were deliberately left to die a slow death, but only after passing on the disease to their spouses and partners, and eventually to their unborn children. Even after the development of penicillin, treatment was never provided until the researchers were busted.

The government did not publicly apologize for this unfortunate tragedy until 1997, when President Clinton made the following apology to the eight remaining survivors. *"The United States government did something that was wrong-deeply, profoundly, morally wrong. It was an outrage to our commitment to integrity and equality for all our citizens...clearly racist* (President Clinton, 1997).

These events have been especially hard for our elders who were more closely connected to the struggle. Therefore, seeking help for psychological problems may be a more difficult task for those who still remember what it was like, back in the day. Our community has always relied on a rich oral history, and the events of the past have been passed down through generations, putting current and future generations on red alert about the potential for ill will on the part of a hostile environment.

You So Crazy

Some African Americans are reluctant to seek help for their psychological problems because they are afraid of the stigma and labels associated with mental illness. There is a negative connotation associated with the terms "mental illness," because of racist events that our people have experienced throughout history. Additionally, the African American community has always believed that *"mental illness"* is synonymous with *"crazy."* Therefore, if you were seeking help for mental problems, you would be considered *"crazy."* You may hear Black folk joke with each other by saying, **"You so Crazy,"** but that is a frightening concept in our community, especially when civil rights workers were placed in mental institutions during peaceful and non-violent demonstrations.

In some Black churches, mental illness is viewed as the result of sin or a lack of faith; so Black people may fail to seek help because of the stigma surrounding mental illness in the church. Therefore, African Americans seek help more often from pastors, physicians, and traditional healers unless mandated to receive professional psychotherapy (term used to refer to talk therapy).

Barrier #3: Misdiagnosis /Medication

African Americans are also distrustful of an institution that is known for misdiagnosing and overmedicating people of color. We are sometimes misdiagnosed because mental health professionals are not knowledgeable and understanding about our cultural world, which serves as a barrier to those in need of mental health services. For example, the research states that African Americans are more likely to receive a diagnosis of Schizophrenia, even though substance abuse may be a more appropriate diagnosis.   This situation happened in the case of Martha.

I Need to Grieve

Martha, a 64 year-old African American grandmother recently learned that her only granddaughter was killed in a drive-by shooting. Martha was devastated, and because she suffered from hypertension, her family rushed her to the emergency room after she collapsed and complained of feeling heaviness and pain in her chest. After a thorough physical examination, the emergency room physician ruled out the presence of heart disease or stroke, and referred Martha to a local community mental health clinic for outpatient treatment.

Martha was taken immediately to the clinic, and during the intake process, the therapist, without taking into consideration Martha's recent trauma or her cultural world, diagnosed her with major depression. She was then referred to a psychiatrist who prescribed Prozac to treat the depression, and an appointment was made for her to see me for individual therapy.

When Martha showed up for the consultation, she was very angry and confused. She explained that she was having a real hard time dealing with her granddaughter's death, but felt even worse because she had not been able to cry since she began taking the Prozac. Martha explained that the medication completely shut her emotions off, and she felt guilty that she had not been able to properly grieve the loss of her granddaughter.

In Martha's cultural world, as in the experience of many African Americans, crying is a very important part of the grieving process when a loved one has passed away. After a thorough evaluation, taking into consideration Martha's cultural world and history, it was determined that she did not meet the criteria for major depression; rather, she appeared to be going through the normal grieving process.

I reported my observations and the results of the assessment to the psychiatrist, modified the diagnosis to "Bereavement," and the Prozac was discontinued. Individuals that fall into the "Bereavement" category exhibit some of the same signs and symptoms of major depression, and these individuals should be monitored. Martha was experiencing depressed mood based on a traumatic event, which usually is a natural reaction to the situation. However, if Martha's grief debilitated her by interfering with her daily functioning, the diagnosis would need to be re-evaluated.

Through culturally relevant therapy focusing on Martha's grief and loss issues, her symptoms of depression began to disintegrate. Martha was on the road to recovery, even though she would always experience feelings of sadness surrounding the loss from time to time.

Martha has learned skills to help her deal with her grief and other stressors more appropriately, which is one of the benefits of psychotherapy. It is important to note, however, if Martha had not been treated by a therapist who understood her cultural world, she would have been treated for the wrong disorder.

I Don't want to take Medication

African Americans are afraid to take medication because they do not always have a good experience. Sometimes they are over medicated, and side effects of various medications may not be adequately explained by physicians. Further, Black folk may not ask about potential side effects, and when they occur, clients freak out and discontinue taking the medication. Since they tend to seek help more often from medical doctors, they will sometimes be prescribed antidepressants without the benefit of getting information about side effects; or they are prescribed medications that are not in their best interest based on our income and/or insurance coverage.

In addition, cultural issues are not always taken into consideration when drugs are prescribed, causing African American clients to have a bad reaction to certain drugs. This cultural ignorance can be especially dangerous to people who are suffering from depression, and at risk of exhibiting suicidal behaviors. Further, Black folk have heard horror stories about medication, so education about the medications that are prescribed might help to relieve some of the inherent stress around this issue.

Barrier #4: Discomfort & Unfamiliarity with Traditional Modalities & Strategies

Some African Americans may not benefit as much from some of the traditional theories, strategies, and techniques as those who are more assimilated into the dominant culture. Therefore, another barrier for Black folk is their discomfort and unfamiliarity with some of the popular treatment approaches we learned in graduate school. While the research is inconclusive, the African Americans I treat tend to benefit more from emic approaches (culturally specific strategies and techniques) that take into consideration individual differences and preferences. According to Western thinking, however, etic approaches (universal approaches, with a one size fit all framework) are overutilized, regardless of the individual's cultural background. When mental health providers use the same strategies and techniques for all their clients, they are bound to make cultural errors.

Barrier #5: Identity Issues and Acculturation

It may be difficult for African Americans to seek help for their problems and/or establish a therapeutic relationship if they are at an incompatible stage of racial/ethnic identity and/or level of acculturation than their therapist, resulting in a poor fit. Our diversity is exhibited by our attitudes, beliefs, and behaviors, which is further reflected in the labels we choose to identify ourselves.

For example, some identify themselves as African American, while others identify themselves as American. When collecting data for my dissertation, in some of the interviews with seniors between the ages of 75 and 80, they shared their concern about being called "African American." After pursuing the conversation further, it was revealed that these elders preferred to be identified as "American" because of the great price their ancestors paid in their fight for freedom.

Therefore, it is critical for mental health providers to acknowledge that there is more than one way to be Black in America. To view every Black person as the same is a huge mistake.

How Many Ways can one be Black?

William E. Cross, Jr. attempted to provide insight on this provocative question through the development of Nigrescence Theory. In the heat of the Black Power Movement in 1971, Cross introduced Nigrescence Theory (a term used to denote the process of becoming Black), a model for understanding the stages of individual Black consciousness development.   Cross (1971) proposed that African Americans progress through a sequence of the following four stages as their racial identity evolved: *Pre-Encounter, Encounter, Immersion-Emersion, and Internalization.*

Cross described *Pre-Encounter* as the stage wherein African Americans devalue his or her own race or racial group and attempt to deny membership in that group. During this stage, the barrier to seeking help may be minimized because these individuals may identify more with the dominant culture. African Americans in this stage of racial identity may be more willing to talk about their problems, and they may actually prefer being treated by Caucasian therapists. But according to Cross, something happens; the individual has an encounter that changes his or her view of the world. African Americans in the *Encounter* stage tend to have experiences that challenge their anti-Black and pro-White attitudes.

We Are all the Same

George was clearly in the Pre-Encounter stage of racial identity development. He had been a corporate manager for the past 10 years, and he lived in a White upper class neighborhood, his kids went to schools in their community, and he and his family socialized primarily with those living in their neighborhood. George believed they were all the same. He and his family were living high on the hog, and he thought he was one of the boys until he was passed over for promotion on three separate occasions. George began to suspect that he was not promoted because of the color of his skin, causing him to file a racial discrimination lawsuit against his employer. After realizing what was happening to him, George became very angry and depressed. He realized, **"WE ARE NOT ALL THE SAME."** George learned that regardless of his status in life, the friendships he had, the house he lived in, and the car he drove, he was still a Black man.

George had an encounter that shook up his core beliefs about White people, and presented cold hard facts about his own Blackness. This revelation made George angry, depressed, anxious, and confused. He even felt a little betrayed, because he fought so hard to maintain his status and to fit into the American fabric. When he was sent to the company psychologist for a psychological evaluation, who was a White woman, George had mixed feelings. In the past, he would have been very comfortable in this setting, but for the first time he realized the huge differences between he and his White colleagues. There was clearly a new barrier developing that may be increasingly difficult to overcome.

In the *Immersion-Emersion* stage, Blacks become more active in the pursuit of their African American cultural heritage. When in this stage, Blacks may feel some measure of anxiety, and Immersion-Emersion attitudes often produce hostile and angry feelings toward the dominant culture. The case of John is an example of Cross' *Immersion-Emersion* stage of racial identity development.

Is it John or Abdul?

John grew up in a primarily White neighborhood, and went to White elementary, middle, and high schools all his life. His father was an attorney and his mother a school teacher. They were determined to make sure John received the best education ever. However, John's parents did everything they could to make sure he had Black friends, so the family worshiped at the local African Methodist Episcopal (AME) Church. John was an excellent student, and he was accepted at U.C. Berkeley immediately after he graduated high school.

John loved Berkeley, and he was very personable and friendly, so he had a lot of friends who were primarily White. Then it happened! John took his first African History course. His interest was peaked immensely, so after completing the history course, he began to take other courses in the Black Studies Department. By the time John finished his third year, he unofficially changed his name from John to

Adbul, wore dread locks, dressed in ethnic garb, and had a new attitude. Abdul was now angry with White people, causing him to dismiss many of the White friends he once hung out with. According to Cross, Adbul's behavior was reflective of the *Immersion-Emersion* stage of racial identity. He fully accepted and valued his Blackness, and deval-ued White America, thereby creating barriers that were difficult to tear down.

When we are in the *Immersion-Emersion* stage, we may be less willing to seek help for our problems, and if we do, we tend to prefer an African American therapist who can understand our cultural world. Interestingly, all African American mental health providers may not fit the bill, since there is more than one way to be Black.

African Americans in the *Internalization* stage tend to internal-ize a positive black identity. *Internalization* attitudes encourage the awareness and acceptance of bicultural identity, which is believed to be important to psychological health. People in this stage realize that there are good people of every ethnic group; therefore some of the barriers to seeking help may be minimized.

I need to pause here long enough to say that barriers not only exist between African American clients and White mental health professionals, because African American therapists may also be incompatible for some African American clients based on competing stages of racial identity. For example, in the case of George, after completing his psychological evaluation with the company psychologist, he became suspicious of her findings, and decided to consult with an African American therapist whose office was close to his home. To his surprise, his experience with the African American therapist was much like that of the White therapist. The therapist was Black on the outside, but she appeared to represent the pro-White stance he was trying to shake, creating even greater barriers to the mental health services he was in need of.

Similarly, cultural barriers may exist when African Americans and therapists are at different levels of acculturation, making it difficult to establish a therapeutic alliance which is critical for the provision of effective mental health services.

In my own research with African Americans, I have found other identity issues that may create cultural barriers. I have identified at least 6 groups that we tend to fit into: African-Centered/ 'Acculturated, Assimilated, Bi-Cultural, Bi-Racial, Sub-Cultural, and Marginalized. These groups are developed based on socialization practices, opportuni-ties to receive acceptance, and experiences with the dominant culture.

African-Centered/Acculturated

According to Parham (2002), "African Centered" is referred to as *"the use of values, customs, traditions, and worldviews as a lens through which our perceptions of reality are shaped and colored."* African-centered individuals tend to express a preference for traditional African principles and values that are demonstrated through values, beliefs, language, foods, practices, rituals, hairstyles, attire, etc. Therefore, the African centered individual may not seek services from providers who do not share their worldview perspective, even if the provider is African American.

Assimilated

Assimilated individuals prefer and fit more comfortably into the dominant culture. Individuals who go to White schools, and live in White neighborhoods tend to share the values of the dominant culture more than those who live in Black enclaves. Sometimes, these individuals view themselves as cultureless, just as do Whites. The assimilated individual may be comfortable receiving mental health services from a European American therapist or a highly assimilated African American therapist.

Bi-Cultural

Bi-Cultural individuals live in two cultures, and they learn to negotiate both in order to survive. W.E.B. Dubois referred to the bi-cultural dilemma as *double consciousness*, because one is forced to live in two worlds, yet not really belonging to either. This may be a lonely place to be, so Black folk code switch (strategy for gaining acceptance in both worlds) by speaking, dressing, and wearing hairstyles that are acceptable in the work setting, and in the hood. The following testimonials will speak to the complexity of the bi-cultural dilemma.

> *There were times ... when I felt a burning sense of shame that I was not with other Blacks - and Whites - standing up to the fire hoses and the police dogs ... As my fame increased, so did my anguish. I knew that many Blacks were proud of my accomplishments on the tennis court. But I also knew that some others ... did not bother to hide ... their disdain and contempt for me.*
>
> **Arthur Ashe, 1993**

> *Like so many other people who have become members of the American society, Negroes have to blend their unique character as a group with the common character they share as Americans. Between these two identifications there has been up to now a deep a mutual split.*
>
> **Harold R. Issacs, 1963, Senior Research Associate, Center for International Studies at Massachusetts Institute of Technology**

> *As a Black professional in American it is sometimes so difficult to find true acceptance in either the black or the white communities that I often feel like an outsider to both; alienation seems to be the price of living with a foot in each world.*
>
> **Lawrence Otis Graham, 1995, President Progressive Management Associates, White Plains, New York**

Those who have been successful in maneuvering through both systems may feel comfortable with either a White or Black therapist.

Bi-Racial

The Bi-Racial group is characterized by double race/ethnicity identification, and this group is very unique because many bi-racial individuals choose one ethnic/racial group to identify with, especially if both parents are not actively in the lives of their bi-racial children. Therefore, their help-seeking behaviors and therapist preferences may depend on the group they identify most heavily with.

Sub-Cultural

We have made the assumption that the barriers to treatment are based solely on issues of race and ethnicity. However, race and ethnicity may have nothing to do with African Americans' cultural preferences when they have group membership in sub-cultural groups, such as religious groups, or even the gang. Therefore, the barriers that exist for African Americans belonging to specific sub-cultural groups may have more to do with mental health professionals' identification with those groups. For example, those belonging to certain religious groups may prefer to be treated by a therapist from their church community.

The research relative to African Americans' preference for a therapist who looks like them has mixed reviews. For example, it is believed that most African Americans who have participated in studies do not have a preference for an ethnically similar therapist. But that is not the case with the clients I serve. The majority of my clients come to me because I am African American with a religious/spiritual background. In my work with these clients, it tends to be most important for them to be treated by someone who can respect them and understand their cultural world.

Barrier #6: Worldview

Barriers may also exist when the client and therapist come from two different worldviews. One's worldview can influence attitudes toward help-seeking, preferences for ethnically similar therapists, and overall attitudes, feelings, and behaviors for the following reasons:

- Worldview represents beliefs, values, and assumptions about people, relationships, nature, time, and activity in our world.
- Worldview effects how we perceive and evaluate situations and how we derive appropriate actions based on our appraisal.
- The nature of clinical reality is also linked to one's worldview.

(Ibrahim, Sodowsky & Ohnishi, 2001; Sue & Sue, 2003)

Barrier #7: Poverty

In addition to all the barriers mentioned above, poverty may be one of the most important barriers to consider. Without adequate financial resources, to provide healthcare to pay for psychological services, and to pay for the appropriate medication, childcare to care for children when their parents come to receive these services, and adequate transportation to get to clinics and other outpatient facilities, some African Americans may be unable to participate in treatment.

Barriers from Therapist's Perspective

We have just discussed some of the barriers that may explain why African Americans continue to suffer in silence. However, it is of equal importance to discuss some of the barriers that may prevent mental health professionals of all ethnic/racial backgrounds from providing effective mental health services to African Americans.

There are five potential barriers from the mental health professional's perspective that must be taken into consideration: Clinician bias, misdiagnoses due to cultural error, discomfort and unfamiliarity with culturally relevant modalities and strategies, acculturation and racial identity issues, and worldview. In this section of the book, you will discover that some African Americans and mental health professionals are faced with similar barriers, but for different reasons. However, the first critical barrier that may get in the way of therapists' providing the most effective services to African Americans is clinician bias.

Barrier #1: Clinician Bias

Clinicians may hold onto negative perceptions, stereotypes and myths that create a bias in the views they hold about African American clients. If therapists believe that Black folk are lazy, angry, and violent, those perceptions will certainly impact the quality of services provided to them. While conducting a focus group with African American clients to understand more about their experiences at a local mental health center, one male client suffering from Schizophrenia made the following observations:

> *"I really do not care about the race of the therapist, I just want them to know they do not need to be afraid of me. I will not hurt them because I have never hurt anyone but myself.*

*I always know my therapist is afraid of me when we're in
the room together, and that is really a bad feeling."*

Some therapists exhibit fear toward Black clients when they have little
contact with Black folk to debunk the erroneous myths and stereotypes
presented by the media.

Barrier #2: Misdiagnoses Due to Cultural Error

Therapists who are unfamiliar with the cultural world of African
American clients may misdiagnose their clients. That's exactly what
happened to Philip. Philip, a 30 year old single father of three was
referred to me after being hospitalized for a homicidal attempt on a
friend he caught trying to sexually molest his 10 year old daughter.
Philip had been diagnosed with Bipolar Disorder five years earlier. By
the time he arrived at my office, Philip was very angry. When I asked
him why he was so angry, he told me his tragic story.

*"I was separated from my children because of my hospitaliza-
tion. After being released, I attempted to get my children
back, so I did whatever they told me to do. I went to see the
therapist that was referred to me and I thought everything was
going well; however, I was wrong. During our time together,
she asked me how I was holding it together and I told her by
taking the medication regularly and by staying connected to
God. She asked me more about my relationship with God, so I
told her that I don't always get to go to church, but I talk to
God everyday. I am sometimes suicidal, and she asked me*

what prevented me from committing suicide, and I told her I hear the voice of God. So when I went to tried to get custody of my children, I was denied because the therapist wrote in my chart that I was hearing voices again, and was too unstable to care for my children."

I asked Philip if he knew the difference between the voice of God and other voices he heard, and he responded positively. Philip explained that he was well aware of the voices he heard when he did not take his medication, and he further explained that he did not hear God speak in an audible voice, rather he experienced the spirit of God. *"The Spirit of God has been my salvation through all I've been through in my life,"* stated Philip.

This story speaks to the heart of why therapists must become more culturally aware, because had Philip's prior therapist understood more about him religious/spiritual worldview, she would have reported more positive information in her report to the court, and she may not have misinterpreted his comments.

Barrier #3: Discomfort & Unfamiliarity with Culturally Appropriate Modalities & Strategies

Therapists of all ethnic backgrounds may be uncomfortable and unfamiliar with culturally appropriate strategies; therefore, they may rely on universal (etic) approaches when working with African American clients, instead of emic approaches (theories developed from individual perspectives, experiences, and practices, all of which are embedded in a particular cultural context Katz, 1985). Counseling and psychotherapy have traditionally been conceptualized in Western, individualistic terms. *"The assumption is that such theories based on this mono cultural perspective are applicable to all populations when they clearly are not* (Katz, 1985)."

Barrier #4: Acculturation and Racial Identity Issues

Just as was demonstrated earlier in this chapter, therapists of all ethnic backgrounds may also be at an incompatible level of acculturation and/or stage of racial/ethnic identity than the client, making it difficult for them to relate to the experiences and issues relevant to African Americans.

Barrier #5: Worldview

As discussed earlier, the therapeutic relationship may be compromised when the therapist and the client come from two different worldviews. Therefore, one of the first steps in providing culturally competent services to African Americans is to first understand more about their racial, ethnic, or cultural background. Many multicultural textbooks provide a section on each of the major ethnic groups, including African Americans, but that information does not necessarily take into consideration the wide diversity that exists within the African American community. Therefore, understanding more about their racial identity, acculturation, and worldview is essential.

So Who is Helping Our People?

If we are not seeking help from mental health professionals, where are we going for help?   Taylor, Hardison & Chatters (1996) suggest we seek help from informal sources, such as friends, family members, and other informal sources, such as beauty salons and barber shops. We also seek help from physicians and traditional healers. In our community, we have traditionally been raised to take care of each other, which has been essential to our survival.   While I think the support sources cited above are valid; they may not always be appropriate to help us to deal with the symptoms of depression and other mental illnesses in our community.

Further, many of us continue to rely on pastors and the Black church as a vital resource for these problems.   However, the sole reliance on the Black church for relief from mental illness may be problematic if the church is not trained to deal with mental health problems. When church folk are taught that seeking professional help for mental, physical, and social problems demonstrates a lack of faith, or if they are taught that traditional psychological and/or medical interventions are inappropriate for Christians, church folk may continue to suffer in silence because they do not want to displease their pastor and/or God.

FOOD FOR THOUGHT

All the barriers from both the potential African American client and mental health professional are important to identify and remove to enable clients to feel more comfortable about seeking help when they are experiencing symptoms of depression and other psychological/emotional distress. I would like to encourage both groups to begin that process as soon as humanly possible. It is not easy for some African Americans to overcome these barriers because they have been constructed in response to a legacy of pain and suffering. In addition, it is not easy for some mental health professionals to overcome their barriers because they have been bombarded by negative images, myths and stereotypes about African Americans throughout history. Further, some of the values they hold near and dear have been promoted by family members and friends they love and trust. But, the process must begin.

So to our community, please give yourselves the opportunity to destroy the barriers that stand between you and your inner healing; and to those who have been called to provide inner healing to our community, please give yourselves the unique opportunity to tear down the walls that stand between you and those you are called to serve. Finally, do not forget to pray and meditate, for God will be with you.

Activity

1. What are some of the barriers that may get in the way of you seeking professional help for problems you may be experienc ing?   If you are a mental health professional, what are some of the barriers that may get in the way of you providing effective services to African American clients?

---

2. What do you need to do in order to destroy the barriers?

MEDITATE ON THESE WORDS

I will love thee, O Lord, my strength. The Lord is my rock, and my fortress, and my deliverer; my God, my strength, in whom I will trust, my buckler, and the horn of my salvation, and my high tower. I will call upon the Lord, who is worthy to be praised: so shall I be saved from mine enemies.

Psalms 18: 1-3KJV

PRAY WITHOUT CEASING

Dear Lord, Please help me to identify the barriers that may prevent me from getting the help I need. Please help me to do the necessary work to destroy these barriers, so that I can experience true inner healing. Amen

Dear Lord, as a mental health provider, I ask your help to identify the barriers that may prevent me from providing the best services to my clients. Please help me to do the necessary work to destroy those barriers, so that I can help the people you have called me to help. Amen

CHAPTER FIVE
BREAKING THE CHAINS THAT BIND

A Spiritual Guide to Inner Healing

How does one break the chains that bind? There is no simple answer to that question. Furthermore, it is not easy to break old habits and change conditions we have grown accustomed to. Nonetheless, in this chapter you will find various strategies that may help you and/or those you care about to successfully break the chains that bind. Many people have been spiritually, mentally, and physically bankrupt for so long, it almost seems like a normal state of being. But they are really screaming on the inside, in the hope that someone will help them. Well, help is on the way.

We have discussed the lethal impact of depression on the African American community. Contrary to the myth that Black folk don't get depressed, we learned our people do suffer with the disease, just like our White counterparts. However, through the love and support of family and friends, a renewed relationship with God, and the culturally competent care of trained mental health professionals, you can and will experience the inner healing and peace you desire. There are six (6) important steps that may be useful in helping you to achieve that goal: (1) Acknowledge the pain; (2) Have a medical consultation; (3) Find a culturally competent mental health professional; (4) Diet and exercise; (5) Seek support; and (6) Renew your relationship with God.

STEP ONE

Acknowledge your Pain

Acknowledging your pain is the first step toward breaking the chains that bind. This is probably the most difficult step to make because we are forced to confront the demon that has us bound. You can do it because you are a survivor, so look straight ahead and don't look back until you've reached the goal. You no longer have to suffer in silence. Remember, all of us at some point or another have suffered or are currently suffering from either acute or chronic emotional/psychological distress.

All of the people you read about in this book had to confront their state of brokenness, and seek help from a trained professional who could understand their issues. I am happy to report, they are all well on their way to putting the pieces of their lives together. In addition, their faith in God and an active prayer life has helped them to successfully go through this process.

MEDITATE ON THESE WORDS

And this is the confidence that we have in him, that, if we ask anything according to his will, he heareth us.

I John 5: 14-KJV

PRAY WITHOUT CEASING

Dear Lord, I thank you so much for bringing me to this point in my life. I do acknowledge my brokenness, and I am asking that you continue to walk with me every step of the way, as I strive to become whole. Amen

STEP TWO

Make an Appointment with your Physician

Once you have acknowledged your condition, it would be a good idea for you to make an appointment with your primary care physician. According to the *National Institute of Mental Health*, you should expect the following from your doctor when consulting him or her regarding your symptoms of depression:

1.   A physical examination to rule out other possible explanations for your symptoms, such as medications and medical conditions. For example, in the case of Janice in Chapter Three, her symptoms very closely resembled those of depression. After further evaluation by her medical doctor, it was discovered she was going through menopause.

2.   Conduct a medication evaluation to determine if anti-

depressants are needed, because they may not be necessary for all persons suffering from depression. Many African Americans do not want to take medication, so it is very important to discuss all concerns with your doctor, and ask questions about possible side effects. Also check to make sure the physician has taken your race/ethnicity into consideration when determining which medication you should take. Some med-ications are better for African Americans than others.

MEDITATE ON THESE WORDS

For we have not a high priest which cannot be touched with the feeling of our infirmities; but was in all points tempted as we are, yet without sin. Let us therefore come boldly unto the throne of grace, that we may obtain mercy, and find grace to help in time of need

Hebrews 4:15-16-KJV

PRAY WITHOUT CEASING

Dear Lord, I am your child, and I am grateful that you are here for me as I continue to seek inner healing. Amen

STEP THREE

Find A Culturally Competent Mental Health Professional

Based on my professional experience and also in my work in the church, there is a need for silent sufferers to seek professional help for their problems. While it is important for African Americans to seek help from pastors, families, and friends, some issues may require professional help.

When does one know when to seek help?

According to information contained in *"A Consumer's Guide to Mental Health Services,"* prepared by the *National Institute of Mental Health Association,* there are several important signs that psychotherapy may be needed:

Prolonged depression (Feelings of sadness for a long period of time)

Thoughts of harming oneself or others

Changes in appetite

Abrupt changes in mood

Irritability and agitation

Undue prolonged anxiety (Excessive nervousness & worry)

Internal or interpersonal conflicts that interfere with functioning

Feelings of low self-esteem and low self-worth

Relationship issues

Finding a culturally competent mental health professional that understands your cultural world is very important in this process. Licensed psychologists, social workers, and marriage and family therapists assist their clients in (1) identifying the problem, (2) identifying the root of the problem; (3) setting realistic goals for treatment; and (4) utilizing culturally appropriate strategies and techniques to reduce negative symptoms and improve their overall quality of life and the quality of their relationships. When necessary, psychologists also conduct psychological testing, assessment, and evaluations. In seeking a culturally competent therapist, make sure he or she possesses some or all of the following characteristics:

The Culturally Competent Therapist

- *Demonstrates empathy for you*
- *Is willing to become the student*
- *Is willing to gain knowledge about the role of spirituality and religion and spirituality in your life*
- *Is comfortable about discussing the impact of racism on your life*
- *Understands why you may be angry and is comfortable in working with your anger*
- *Is open to learning about your acculturation level, stage of racial identity and/or worldview*
- *Considers the within group differences that exist among African Americans, and assesses who you are before jumping to conclusions about your needs and preferences*
- *Is willing to gain an understanding of cultural paranoia*
- *Is desirous of establishing a healthy therapeutic alliance with you*
- *Has the ability to create a warm and empathic environment*
- *Allows you to share your story, which includes your history, cultural identity, needs, strengths, and resources*
- *Demonstrates respect for you through active listening and timing*
- *Does not expect you to open up immediately, and demonstrates understanding and patience*
- *Does not jump to conclusions about you too quickly*
- *Allows you to give your explanation of the problem*
- *Becomes your advocate*

Culturally Competent therapists use the following therapeutic strategies and techniques that takes African Americans' cultural context into account:

1.   ***Adlerian Therapy*** because this approach teaches providers to use their skills to encourage clients through active listening, empathy, respect, optimism, and faith;

2.   ***Multisystems Model*** that encourages providers to intervene with Black families at multiple levels, including the individual, the family, the extended family, church, community networks, and the social service system;

3.   ***Narrative Therapy*** which allows clients to reconstruct their story and create a new one;

4.   ***Group Therapy*** because African Americans are accustomed to working together in small groups; and they may feel more comfortable about sharing their problems with those who have similar struggles.

Integration of Traditional Strategies with Christian Principles

African Americans Christians should look for therapists who are able to effectively integrate traditional strategies with Christian principles. For example, therapists who effectively integrate Cognitive Behavioral Therapy with Christian values and beliefs may seek to achieve the following goals:

1.   Help clients identify, challenge, confront and modify maladaptive thoughts, feelings, and beliefs based on misperceptions regarding sin;

2.   Help clients deal with guilt;

3.   Incorporate prayer;

4.   Introduce the importance of forgiveness to achieve inner healing.

Back Down Memory Lane

Remember, Sharon, the young lady with all the rage? Well, she is doing much better today because she was able to identify, challenge and confront maladaptive thoughts surrounding the abuse she experienced as a child. Sharon gave herself permission to place blame where it belonged (onto the perpetrator), and to begin the process of forgiving the perpetrator, which has virtually changed her life in a positive way. Sharon is taking an antidepressant for the depression, which has decreased her depressed mood. Further, I obtained permission from Sharon to include her pastor's wife as a member of her support team, which has enabled her to feel more comfortable about receiving mental health treatment.

Without receiving culturally competent treatment Sharon's life may have been ruined. Had she continued to suffer in silence without support, she would have been more at risk of committing suicide. Further, Sharon may have continued to maintain the faulty belief that she was too broken to be fixed.

Where will I find the right Therapist?

In choosing a culturally competent therapist, it is important to seek referrals from your family, friends, church family, or professional organizations, such as the *Association of Black Psychologists (ABPSI)*. Once you have located a potential therapist, it is also important to check his or her credentials, and to ask questions about the method of treatment, length of treatment, and the professional's thoughts about your particular problem. Furthermore, ask the therapist about their experience in working with clients with similar problems, coming from similar cultural backgrounds.

MEDITATE ON THESE WORDS

The Lord is my light and my salvation; whom shall I fear? The Lord is the strength of my life; of whom shall I be afraid? When the wicked and even mine enemies came upon me to eat up my flesh they stumbled and fell. Though an host should encamp against me, my heart shall not fear: though war should rise against me, in this will I be confident.

Psalms 27:1-3-KJV

PRAY WITHOUT CEASING

Dear Lord, I am preparing to make a big step in my life. Please lead and direct me as I seek to choose a culturally competent therapist who will understand my needs. I am somewhat afraid, so please go before me. Amen.

STEP FOUR

Diet and Exercise

The research is quite clear about the benefits of diet and exercise in decreasing depressed mood. Also, you will greatly benefit from regular rest and relaxation. These are gifts you must give yourself in order to be psychologically healthy. Failure to eat properly and exercise, and get enough rest and relaxation will not serve you well, especially because of all the stressors that are beyond your control. If you really want to be repaired, you must do the necessary work to participate in the process.

Self-Care Covenant

Make a commitment to take better care of yourself, because if you do not, no one else will. Make a covenant with yourself, write it down where you can see it each day, and adhere to what you agree upon. However, if you are unable to reach your daily goals, forgive yourself, and begin again the next day. Solicit the support of a loved one or friend.

1. Today I will give up one unhealthy thing in my life.
2. Today I will write a plan that includes healthy eating and exercise after conferring with my primary care physician.
3. Today I will make plans to build in relaxation each week (e.g., take a long hot bath or get a massage).
4. Today I will affirm myself.
5. Today I will take time to pray and meditate on God's Word.

STEP FIVE

Seek Support

Everyone needs someone, and this is especially true for people suffering from debilitating depressive disorders. You need family and friends around you for support and care. However, it is important to carefully select those persons you wish to be your supporters. Sometimes, negative supporters (e.g., family and friends) can bring you further down, so select people who have a positive outlook on life, rather than those who are negative themselves. Surround yourself with people of faith, who are hopeful, and understand the power of prayer and faith. If you are suffering from depression, or any disease, you need praying people around you.

The African American church is a great source of strength and support in the community. Many churches have support groups and other small group activities that can encourage and uplift you. However, you must be careful with church groups, because sometimes negativity can creep into the church, and invade those small groups. So again, find people who can love and care for you, and provide positive support when you need it.

STEP SIX

Reconnect to the Spirit

For many African Americans, inner healing is virtually impossible if we fail to reconnect to the spirit. In their book, "Black Man Emerging, " Dr. Joseph White and Dr. James Cones, III remind us of the importance of the Spiritual connection for African Americans: *"African existence is deeply spiritual. There is a deep-seated belief that a creative, life-affirming force controlled by God permeates the universe. "* This component of the healing process is critical because as you reconnect to the spirit of God, you will experience optimal health and wholeness. I believe there are 5 components that are necessary for us to reconnect to the Spirit: (1) Understand your Purpose, (2) Pray and Meditate, (3) Forgive; (4) Love; and (5) Praise and Worship.

Understand Your Purpose

I have been reading an exciting and uplifting book entitled, "The Purpose Driven Life, " by Rick Warren. Readers take a 40-day journey during which time, they are given the awesome opportunity to discover their purpose and develop faith. After reading the book, you will know and understand whnat your purpose on earth is. Black people have struggled in so many ways, but our strong faith and belief in God have helped us to survive. However, some of us have bought into the world's system that promotes individualism, and the acquisition of stuff and things because we don't know our purpose on earth. When we are unable to live up to the world's standards, we become sick. So Rick Warren helps us to reconnect to the spirit through gaining a better understanding of our true purpose on earth. According to Warren:

Knowing your purpose gives meaning to your life
Knowing your purpose simplifies your life
Knowing your purpose focuses your life
Knowing your purpose motivates your life
Knowing your purpose prepares you for eternity…

MEDITATE ON THESE WORDS

You Lord, give perfect peace to those who keep their purpose firm and put their trust in you.

Isaiah, 26:3-KJV

PRAY WITHOUT CEASING

Dear Lord, help me to discover my purpose so I will know why I am here and what I am supposed to do while I am here. Thank you for choosing me. Amen

Prayer and Meditation

I hope you have benefited from the prayers and meditations that were provided for you throughout the book. Prayer and meditation are extremely important for reconnecting to the spirit and achieving inner healing. We must pray without ceasing. Research studies have shown that prayer has a very positive effect on people suffering from both physical and psychological disabilities, so prayer and meditation will be helpful to you as you go through the healing process.

Forgive and Let Go

It is impossible to reconnect to the Spirit without a forgiving heart. Many of us suffer from depression and other psychological and physical illnesses because we have a difficult time forgiving those who have hurt us. Forgiveness is a spiritual concept, and if we do not forgive each other, we will continue to suffer from a broken heart. Forgiveness is very difficult because it implies that when we forgive the person who wronged us, we are letting him or her off the hook. However, when we truly forgive, we are letting ourselves off the hook. We must give ourselves permission to forgive because it is a gift we extend to those who may not deserve it. When you give a real gift, you do not ask for anything in return; and that is the way we must forgive each other, especially since the other person may never acknowledge they were wrong.

I believe, however, that the most important act of forgiveness is when we forgive ourselves. There are people who are broken and in despair because they fail to forgive themselves for having an abortion, getting a divorce, disappointing family members, and even disappointing God. Forgive yourself and others. **LET IT GO!** Begin to enjoy the good health and happiness you so richly deserve.

In his book, *"When Forgiveness Doesn't Make Sense,"* Robert Jeffress gives four reasons why we should choose forgiveness over vengeance:

Forgiveness is the only way to settle a debt
Forgiveness frees us to get on with our lives
Forgiveness is an antidote to needless suffering
Forgiveness is the obligation of the forgiven

Activity

1.   After spending time in prayer and meditation so that God can prepare your heart for forgiveness, write a letter to someone you need to forgive, even if the person is you.

   •*Remind the person how they hurt you.*
   •*Tell them how the act or deed has made you feel.*
   •*Tell them how the act or deed has impacted your life.*
   •*And if you can, tell the person you forgive him or her, so the person will no longer have power over your life.*

It is up to you to do what you want with the letter. Perhaps you wish to mail it to the person (even if the person is you). But, you may wish to have a symbolic ceremony, where you burn the letter, or tear the letter into pieces, or some other symbolic act that will help you to let it go. You may even wish to bury the letter, **JUST DO NOT DIG IT UP AGAIN!**

2.   After spending time in prayer and meditation, write a letter to someone you have hurt.

   •*Remind the person how you hurt them.*
   •*Tell them how it has made you feel to have offended them.*
   •*Tell them how the wrongful deed has impacted your life.*
   •*And if you can, tell them you are sorry.*

Follow the same instructions cited above, but this time, you have the opportunity to send the letter to the person, or create some other symbolic way to rid yourself of the guilt associated with the deed. Remember, the goal of this activity is to forgive yourself and others so you can be reconnected to the spirit and continue on the road to inner healing.

MEDITATE ON THESE WORDS

Dearly beloved, avenge not yourselves, but rather give place unto wrath: for it is written, Vengeance is mine; I will repay, saith the Lord. Therefore, if thine enemy hunger, feed him; if he thirst, give him drink: for in doing so thou shalt heap coals of fire on his head

Romans: 12:19-21-KJV

PRAY WITHOUT CEASING

Dear Lord, please help me to forgive those who have hurt me, and most of all, please help me to forgive myself and let it go. Amen

What's Love Got to Do with It?

Tina Turner asked the question: *"What's love got to do with it?"* I'm sure you will agree that love has everything to do with it, and reconnecting to the Spirit is also impossible without love. Unfortunately, some of us are neither free to love, nor free to receive love because of heavy baggage from the past. However, Maya Angelou addressed this issue:

Someone was hurt before you, wronged before you, beaten before you, humiliated before you, raped before you, yet someone survived.

You may be saying to yourself, *"What is she talking about? I know how to love!"* Well, I believe some of us really do not know how to love because of the type of love we received growing up, and past experiences of hurt and trauma. Unfortunately, some of us have not had the benefit of observing love modeled for us, so love may need to be redefined.

So, what is love? Wilferd Peterson describes love this way: *"Love is the dove of peace, the spirit of brotherhood and sisterhood, it is tenderness and compassion, forgiveness and tolerance, love is the supreme good, it is the overflowing life, the giving of ourselves to noble ends and causes; love is down to earth, and it reaches to the highest star, it is the valley of humility and the mountaintop of ecstasy. Love is the spiritual magnetism that draws men and women together for the working of miracles."*

Carlyle wrote, *"Ten persons banded together in love could do what ten thousand separately would fail in. Love is the perfect antidote that floods the mind to wash away hatred, jealousy, resentment, anxiety, and fear. Love alone can release the power of the atom so it will work for man and not against him. Love in the words of the Master, is the shining commandment, Love one another."*

It is difficult for broken people to love, for they have tucked love away in a safe place because they are afraid. But love is waiting to be dug up, and it all starts with the love of God. So if you really want to be healed on the inside, you must love and receive God's love.

"Though I speak with the tongues of men and angels, and have not love, I am become as sounding brass, or a tinkling cymbal. And though I have the gift of prophecy, and understand all mysteries, and all knowledge; and though I have all faith, so that I could remove mountains, and have not love, I am nothing. And though I bestow all my goods to feed the poor, and though I give my body to be burned, and have not love, it profiteth me nothing. But the 13th verse states, and now abideth faith, hope, love, these three, but the greatest of these is love."

I Corinthians 13:1-3 - KJV

Remember, the art of love is God at work through you, and without it, you will not be connected to the spirit of God, for God is love!

Activity

1.   Write a love letter to Jesus to help you develop that special relationship with him.

2.   Write a love letter to yourself, because you must love yourself in order for you to love others. Jesus said, *"Love your neighbor as yourself."*

3.   Now write a love letter to someone you need to demonstrate your love to, and send it to him or her.

MEDITATE ON THESE WORDS

For God so loved the world that He gave His only begotten son that whosoever believeth in Him should not perish, but have everlasting life.

John 3:16-KJV

PRAY WITHOUT CEASING

Dear Lord, thank you for allowing me to experience your love. Help me to demonstrate agape love to others. Amen

Getting My Praise On

One sure way to reconnect to the spirit is to participate in daily praise and worship; however, we are sometimes too broken to give Him praise or to worship Him. The Lord loves the praises of His people, so we just ought to praise Him, because He is worthy. I encourage you to read Richard Foster's book, *"Celebration of Discipline,"* that admonishes us to participate in the inward disciplines (meditation, prayer, fasting, and study); the outward disciplines (simplicity, solitude, submission, and service); and lastly, the corporate disciplines; (confession, worship, guidance, and celebration) Sometimes, we have to praise him even when we are broken and feeling down and out.   In Exodus 15:20, Miriam led the children out of Israel into a victory celebration because God delivered them out of the hands of the enemy. Well, God is trying to deliver you from your state of brokenness, so while you're waiting, go ahead and **GET YOUR PRAISE ON!**

Activity

1.   Write down three things God has done for you lately.

_____

_____

_____

_____

**Now take time to give Him praise and worship
for who He is, and for all the great things He has done!**

MEDITATE ON THESE WORDS

Praise ye the Lord Praise God in his sanctuary; praise him in the firmament of his power. Praise him for his mighty acts; praise him according to his excellent greatness. Praise him with the sound of the trumpet; praise him with the psaltery and harp. Praise him with the timbre and dance; praise him with stringed instruments and organs. Praise him upon the loud cymbals; praise him upon the high sounding cymbals. Let everything that hath breath praise the Lord Praise ye the Lord.

Psalms 150-KJV

PRAY WITHOUT CEASING

Dear Lord, please accept my praise and worship to you, for you deserve all glory, honor, and praise. Amen.

EPILOGUE
PASSING IT ON

Our people have experienced tremendous pain and suffering, but we are resilient and strong, and we have been successful in overcoming great adversity throughout history. However, we may not be strong enough to overcome the negative effects of depression and other psychological disorders without professional help, a strong connection with God, and the love and support of family, friends, the church, and the community. It is my sincerest hope that this book has helped you or someone you love to begin and/or continue the healing process. If you have begun your journey toward inner healing, your life will never be the same, but now you have the awesome responsibility to **PASS IT ON**. It was too late for Frank, the young man we read about in the Introduction of this book, but it does not have to be too late for you and/or those you love and care about.

When we Know Better, we Should do Better

We all learned some things through the tragic circumstances of Frank's death, and because of the pastor's response, other broken people were able to receive healing through help from trained professionals and their spiritual connection with God. The big "D" (depression) word is now out in Frank's church, and the pastor has made the commitment to ensure that his people become educated about mental illness and they are encouraged to seek professional help when needed.

The church leadership is now much more aware of some of the warning signs associated with suicide and have made this information available to all parishioners. *Hope Allianz Inc, Counseling and Health Center* distributed important warning signs for suicide risk. According to this report, the following situations and circumstances increase individuals risk of committing suicide:

• The individual has attempted suicide before
• A family member has successfully committed suicide
• The individual takes unnecessary risks that might be life threatening or dangerous
• The individual has had a recent severe loss or losses
• The individual loses interest in their personal appearance
• The individual increases alcohol and/or drug use
• The individual is a young Black male, especially between the ages of 10-14.

Warning Signs for Suicide Risk
Published by
Hope Allianz, Inc. Counseling and Healing Center

http://www.hopeallianz.com

- The individual is talking or joking about suicide (e.g., committing suicide themselves or talking about it in general).
- The individual is preoccupied with death and dying (e.g., recurrent death themes in music, literature, drawings, writing letters or leav ing notes referring to death or "the end").
- The individual is making statements about being reunited with a deceased loved one.
- The individual has trouble eating and sleeping.
- The individual experiences drastic changes in their behavior.
- The individual withdraws and isolates from family, friends, or social activities.
- The individual loses interest in things they care about (e.g., hobbies, work, school).
- The individual prepares for death by making out a will and making final arrangements as if to set one's affairs in order.
- The individual gives away personal possessions.
- The individual is making statements about hopelessness, helpless ness, or worthlessness (for example, "Life is useless." "Everyone would be better off without me." "It does not matter, I won't be around much longer anyway." I wish I could just disappear").
- The individual becomes suddenly happier and calmer.
- The individual makes unusual visits or calls to people they care about...saying their good-byes.
- The individual participates in self-destructive behaviors (e.g., alco hol or drug abuse, self-injury or manipulation, promiscuity).
- The individual participates in risk-taking behaviors (e.g., reckless driving or excessive speeding, carelessness around bridges, cliffs or balconies, or walking in front of traffic).

The 2003 *U.S. Surgeon General's Report* revealed that suicide rates among young Black males between the ages of 10-14 has increased by 233%.   Therefore, if your loved one is exhibiting any of the warning signs listed above, it may be useful to seek help from a trained professional. Sometimes, the warning signs are not very clear, so if the person possesses some of the risk factors, and he or she is unwilling to seek help from a trained professional, call 911. The police department will assist you by sending out a team of professionals who can assess the situation, and refer you appropriately. Also, feel free to contact the suicide hotline listed below.

NATIONAL SUICIDE HOTLINE
1-800-SUICIDE

Frank's pastor and the leadership team have also developed a counseling ministry in their church, led by trained professionals. The pastor now believes the combination of both traditional and spiritual strategies are sometimes necessary to help people to achieve inner healing, and he gives people permission to seek help for their problems both inside and outside the church walls. This incident has had an enormous impact on the pastor of the church, which has greatly benefited the body of Christ.

Sandra and the children are in family counseling to help them cope with grief and loss issues. They are also participating in a support group with other families who have suffered similar losses. It is not unusual for surviving family members to experience feelings of guilt when their loved one commits suicide, and for a long time, Sandra believed she should have been able to prevent Frank's death. However, she learned through participating in group therapy with others experiencing similar grief and loss issues, that nothing or no one could have prevented Frank from taking his life. Suicide is one of the possible consequences of untreated depression.

I left the funeral that day even more committed to help our people to overcome their state of brokenness. I also left with a greater zeal to pass on what I know to: (1) educate our people about mental illness; (2) eliminate some of the cultural barriers; (3) help them understand more about the lethal effects of mental illness on their personal, professional, and spiritual lives; and (4) introduce culturally relevant treatment interventions, (psychological and spiritual), to prevent Frank's story from being relived in our community. I believe these goals were accomplished through the information shared in this book.

Over the past two years, there have been three separate suicides in our small community where the victims were active members of local churches. When these tragedies struck our community, it wasn't long before we began to talk about depression in a real way. I shudder to think that it took the deaths of three precious individuals to encourage this long overdue dialogue between the church, mental health professionals, and the community at large.

In my work with clients, and in my experience as co-pastor of an African American church, I have watched the negative impact of depression in the lives of our people. Both in and out of the church, some people who present with symptoms of depression (e.g., irritable mood, abrupt changes in mood, and interpersonal conflicts) may be labeled as trouble makers; when in actuality they are really troubled and broken people in need of repair. However, the church can serve as a powerful resource to help broken people when the church more fully acknowledges and understands mental illness.

I do believe that God is our ultimate source for inner healing, and that He does answer prayer. However, God delights in using His people to help people who are in need. Our people have survived the atrocities of slavery, racism, discrimination, poverty, and other social ills because of our strong faith and belief in God. However, failure to acknowledge the need for medication or talk therapy (talking about your problems with a trained professional), for disabling diseases like depression, may lead to other mental and physical problems and ultimately death.

Black pastors continue to serve as important gatekeepers for their flocks, and I am convinced they are concerned about their people's physical, psychological and spiritual well-being. In fact, many of those I treat would not have sought help for their problems had I not been introduced and embraced by the church community. And some of my clients would not have sought help from any mental or physical health care provider regardless of the provider's ethnic, racial, or cultural background, without the blessings of their pastor.

Many Black pastors are *Passing it On*, by providing education about mental illness, and giving permission to parishioners to seek outside help when they need it. These pastors are also realizing that sermons and teachings must include practical solutions to real life issues and situations. Furthermore, pastors are becoming much more aware that hurting and broken people are sitting in the pews, and they are developing more sensitivity and tolerance for individuals who may act out because they are in pain.

So, the question remains, how can you *Pass it On?* You can Pass it On, by acknowledging your brokenness, and seeking professional help for it. Failure to admit your pain and suffering will lead to psychological and physical problems. Once you are well on your way to inner healing, you can *Pass it On* by openly sharing your experiences of depression or other psychological problems with family, friends, and church family, to help remove the stigma and shame surrounding mental illness. Your testimony can be of great benefit to those who continue to sit in silence while broken and in pain. We discussed some of the reasons we may fail to talk about our brokenness. However, I am convinced that people may also fail to talk about their problems because they do not want anyone to know the horrible things that have happened to them. So, if you become willing to share your story in a safe environment, others may become willing to seek help.

But more important, you can *Pass it On* by creating a healthy environment for your children to insulate them from the lethal effects of mental illness. We did not discuss depression among children and youth, but we are seeing more and more depressed young people. As stated earlier, the suicide rates among young Black males have risen sharply over the past decade.

Therefore, we must pay more attention to the needs of our young people, and make sure they are not misdiagnosed and/or labeled with ADHD or conduct disorder. According to the *DSM-IV*, children and youth who are depressed tend to exhibit acting out behaviors that resemble ADHD and conduct disorder. Thus, it may be helpful for you to learn more about mental wellness in order to **Pass it On** to your children.

We also need to create a home environment where children are guaranteed to receive nurturance and love. Many of us work real hard to make sure our children have more than we did. But this thinking may be problematic because children need to spend quality time with their parents, instead of spending quality time with television, video games, and friends who may not be the best substitute for you. Families are spending less and less time together in search of the American dream, resulting in broken marriages and broken children who are forced to suffer in silence because we are not there for them.

We must also work harder to rebuild a true sense of community, for it has been altered. Some of us have bought into the world's system that promotes the idea of individualism, competition, and capitalism, which may not always be compatible with the promotion of health and well-being for our community.

W.E.B. DuBois warned us to avoid "*vulgar careerism*" a term used when we focus on individual success and/or self-advancement. In the context of this statement, DuBois was speaking about Black folk's obligation to the advancement of all Black people. However, in the context of this book, I am using the term to admonish us to avoid becoming so caught up in keeping up with the "*Jone's*" that we no longer rec-

ognize our children and spouses, and our commitment to the community. It just might be time for you and I to re-evaluate our priorities if
we are going to promote mental wellness.

Benefits of Inner Healing

There are several exciting benefits associated with being healed on the
inside:

1. Your life will take on new meaning with a new outlook on life.
2. Your family will be blessed.
3. Your goals and aspirations will be achieved.
4. Important relationships will be restored, and new relationships
   will be developed.
5. You will begin to feel and look good.
6. You will be willing and able to pass it on
7. You will be free.

A Message to my Brothers and Sistahs

It takes courage to confront your problems, but you will never
regret the decision to become healed. As you go through your process,
your sons and daughters will be watching. Teach your children who
they are, where they come from, why they're here, and the awesome
responsibility that has been placed on their shoulders. The greatest gift
you can give them is a warm, loving, and nurturing environment, where
healthy people abide, where people love and respect one another, and
where God reigns supreme.

You may be afraid to tell anyone about your problems, and that is certainly understandable based on our history in this country. But solicit the help of family and friends for resources to help you find professional help, because if you continue to remain broken and in despair, that is the legacy you will leave for your children, and generations to come. Remember, God knows your struggle, and even though He sometimes seems very far away, He is with you, and He will be with you always.

But in the meantime, make time to go back to church and become active. Take time for long walks, and soothing baths by candlelight. Find ways to refresh your mind, body, and spirit, so that the healing virtue of God can enter in. And if anyone asks you, "**ARE YOU TOO BROKEN TO BE FIXED?**" I pray your answer will be a resounding **NO**.

RESOURCES

These resources may be helpful to you, a family member or friend if the need arises.

American Psychological Association
750 First Street, NE
Washington D.C. 20002-4242
(800) 374-2721
www.apa.org

Association of Black Psychologists (ABPSI)
P.O. Box 55999
Washington D.C. 20040-5999
(202) 722-0808
www.abpsi.org

Black Psychiatrist of America
C/o Ramona Davis, M.D.
866 Carlston Avenue
Oakland, CA 94610
(510) 834-7103
www.blackpsychiatristofamerica.com

National Alliance for the Mentally Ill
Colonial Place Three
2107 Wilson Blvd., Ste. 300
Arlington, VA 22201
1-800-950-NAMI or 703-524-7600
www.nami.org

National Black Women's Health Project
600 Pennsylvania Avenue SE, Suite 310
Washington DC 20003
(202) 548-4000
www.nationalblackwomenshealthproject.org

National Domestic Violence Hotline
800-799-7233

National Institute of Mental Health
(NIMH) 5600 Fishers Lane, Room 7-99
Rockville, MD 20857
(888) ANXIETY
www.nimh.nih.gov/anxiety

National Mental Health Association
1021 Prince Street
Alexandria, VA 22314-2971
(800) 969-nmha
www.nmha.org

National Suicide Hotline
1-800-SUICIDE

Rape, Abuse, Incest National Network
800 656-HOPE

SELECTED BIBLIOGRAPHY

American Psychiatric Association. (1994). *The diagnostic and statistical manual of mental disorders* (4th ed.). Washington, DC.

Ani, M (1994). *Yurugu: An African Centered Critique of European Cultural Thought and Behavior.* Trenton: African World Press.

Bass, B.A., costa, F.X., & Evans, L.A. (1982). *The* Black American patient. In F.X. Acosta, J. Yamamota, & L.A. Evans (Eds), *Effective Psychotherapy for Low-Income and Minority Patients* (pp. 83-108), New York: Plenum.

Beck, A.T. (1976) *Cognitive therapy and the emotional disorders.* New York: International Universities Press.

Broman, C. (1993). Race differences in marital well-being. *Journal of Marriage and the Family*, 55, 724-732.

Brown, T.N., Sellers, S.L., Brown, K.T., & Jackson, J.S. (1999). Race, ethnicity, and culture in the sociology of mental health. In C.S. (Aneshensel & J.C. Phelan (Eds.), *Handbook of the Sociology of Mental Health* (pp. 167-182). New York NY: Kluwer Academic/Plenum Publishers.

Buechner, F. (1993). *Wishful thinking: A seeker's ABC.* San Francisco: Harper.

Clark, M.O. *Untreated, untold: African Americans with depression.* UCLA Women's Writers Workshop, February, 1998.

Coryell, W., Endicott, J., Andreasen, N.C., & Keller, M. (1985). Bipolar I, bipolar II, and nonbipolar major depression among the relatives of affectively ill probands. *American Journal of Psychiatry*, 142, 817-821.

Cross, W.E. Jr. (1971, July). The Negro-to-Black conversion experience. *Black World*, pp. 13-27.

Cross, T.L. Bazron, B.J., Dennis, K.W., Issacs, M.R., & Benjamin, M.P. (1989). *Toward a culturally competent system of care* (Volume I). Washington, DC: National Technical Assistance Center for Children's Mental Health.

Culbertson, F.M. (1997). Depression and gender: An international review. *American Psychologist*, 52(1), 25-31.

Dana, R.H., Behn, J.D., & Gonwa, T. (1992). A checklist for the
    examination of cultural competence in social services agencies.
Research on Social Work Practice, 2(2).

Du Bois, W.E.B. (1903). *The souls of Black folks.* Chicago: McClurg.

Du Bois, W.E.B. (1899). *The Philadelphia Negro*: A social study.

Ellison, C.G. (1998). Religion, health, and well-being among African
    Americans, 4(1), *African American Research Perspective*, 1-8.

Foster, R. (1983). *Celebration of discipline.* San Francisco: Harper.

Franklin, A.J. (1999). Invisibility syndrome and racial identity
    development in psychotherapy and counseling African American
men. *Counseling Psychologist*, 27, 6, 761-793.

Harrell, S. P. (2000). A multidimensional conceptualization of racism-
    related stress: Implications for the well-being of people of color.
    American Journal of Orthopsychiatry, 70, 42-57.

Hudson, H.M. & Stern, H.(2000). *The heart of the matter.* Roscoe, Il.:
    Hilton Publishing.

Ibrahim, F.A., Roysircar-Sodowsky, G., & Ohnishi, H. (2001).
    Worldview: Recent developments and needed directions. In
    J.G. Ponterotto, M.C. Cases, L.A. Suzuki, and C.M. Alexander
    (Eds), *Handbook of Multicultural Counseling* (2nd Ed), (pp.
    425-455). Thousand Oaks: Sage Publishing.

Jeffress, R. (2000). *When forgiveness doesn't make sense.* Colorado:
    Waterbrook Press.

Katz, J. (1985). The sociopolitical nature of counseling. *The Counseling
    Psychologist.* 13(4), 615-624.

Keith, V., and Norwood, R.S. (1997). Marital strain and depressive
    symptoms among African Americans. *African American
    Research Perspectives*, 3(2), 7-11.

Kohn, L.P. & Hudson, K.M. (2002). Gender, ethnicity, and depression:
    Intersectionality and context in mental health research
    with African American women. *African American
    Research Perspective*, 8(1), 174-184.

Kunjufu, J. (1990). *Countering the conspiracy to destroy Black boys.*
    Chicago, Il: African-American Images.
    Life Application Bible (1989) King James Version,
    Tyndale House Pub.

Martin, M. (2002). *Saving our last nerve.* Roscoe, Il: Hilton Publication

Maxmen, J.S. & Ward,N.G. (1995). *Essential psychopathology and its treatment,* (2nd ed.), New York, NY: W.W. Norton & Co. (p.219)

Morrow, G. (2005). Strengthening the Ties that Bind: A guide to a healthy marriage. Pomona, CA: Shining Glory Publications, Inc. Morrow, G.P., Penn, N.E., & Mouttapa, M. (in review). *A research critique of African American acculturation.*

Neal-Barnett, A. (2003). *Soothe your nerves: The Black woman's guide to understanding and overcoming anxiety, panic, & fear.* New York, N.Y.: Simon & Shuster.

Parham, T.A. (2002). *Counseling persons of African descent: Raising the bar of practitioner competence.* Thousand Oaks: Sage.

Parham, T.A. (1999). Invisibility syndrome in African descent people: Understanding the cultural manifestations of the struggle for self-affirmation. *Counseling Psychologist,* 27, 6, 794-801.

Parham, T.A. & White, J.L. (1990). *The psychology of Blacks.* Upper Saddle River, N.J.: Prentice Hall.

Pervin, L.A. & John, O.P. (2001). *Personality theory and research,* (8th ed.), New York: John Wiley & Sons, Inc.

Peterson, W. (1993). *The art of living.* New York, N.Y.: Galahad Books.

Plomin, R. (1994). *Genetics and experience: The interplay between nature and nurture.* Newbury Park, CA: Sage.

Queener, J.E., & Martin, J.K. (2001). Providing culturally relevant mental health services: Collaboration between psychology and the African American church. *Journal of Black Psychology,* 27, 1, 112-122.

Roy, B. (1995). The Tuskegee syphilis experiment: Biotechnology and the administrative state. *Journal of the National Medical Association,* 87, 56-67.

Stewart, C.F. III. (1999). *Black spirituality and Black consciousness: Soul force, culture and freedom in the African-American experience.* Trenton, New Jersey: African World Press.

Sue, D. W., & Sue, D. (2003). *Counseling the culturally diverse: Theory and practice* (4th ed.). New York: John Wiley & Sons, Inc.

Taylor, R.J., Hardison, C.B., & Chatters, L.M. (1996). Kin and nonkin as sources of informal assistance, In H.W. Neighbors & J.S. Jackson's (Ed), *Mental Health in Black America* (pps. 130-145). Thousand Oaks: Sage.

Utsey, S.Q. (1998). Assessing the stressful effects of racism: A review of instrumentation. *Journal of Black Psychology*, 24, 3, 269-288. Utsey, S.Q., Ponterotto, J.G., Reynolds, A.L., & Cancelli, A.A. (2000). Racial discrimination, coping, life satisfaction, and self-esteem among African Americans. *Journal of Counseling and Development*, 78, 1, 72-80.

Warren, R. (2002). *The purpose driven life.* Grand Rapids, Mi: Zondervan.

White, J.L., & Cones, J.H. (1991). *Black man emerging.* New York, N.Y.: W.H. Freeman & Co.

Williams, D.R., Williams-Morris, R. (2000). Racism and mental health: The African American experience. *Ethnicity and Health,* 5, 243-264.

Wyatt, G.E. (1999). Beyond invisibility of African American males: The effects on women and families. *Counseling Psychologist,* 27, 6, 802-809.

Yeh, C.J. (1999). Invisibility and self-construal in African American men: Implications for training and practice. *Counseling Psychologist,* 27, 6, 810-819.

INTERNET SOURCES

www.blackhealth.com

www.blackwomenshealth.org/site/PageServer

www.cabwhp.org

www.census.gov

www.healthyplace.com/communities/depression/minorities_9asp

www.hopeallianz.com/ResourceCenter/Suicide6_warningsigns.html

www.mentalhealth.org/cre/ch3_historical_context.asp. Minorities
&
Mental Health Report of the U.S. Surgeon General

www.mentalhealth.org/cre/fact1.asp

www.psychologytoday.com/htdocs/prod/PTOArticle/
PTO-20030930-000001.asp. Psychology Today's Blues Buster
Newsletter (September 30, 2003)

www.womensenews.org/article.cfm/dyn/aid/1392/context/archive

INDEX

Additional Books by
Dr. Gloria Morrow

**STRENGTHENING THE TIES THAT BIND: A GUIDE TO A
HEALTHY MARRIAGE**

By Dr. Gloria Morrow

Dr. Morrow discusses some of the challenges that married couples
face as well as strategies for strengthening their marriages.
The book contains activities for couples to help them to begin the
process of healing their marital relationships.

THE THINGS THAT MAKE MEN CRY

By Dr. Gloria Morrow

Dr. Morrow conducted extensive and intimate interviews with 20 men
who share their stories of manhood and fatherhood, and the things
they want to say to their women. These brave men explore and discuss the issues that make them, and other men cry both internally and
externally. This book will be available Summer 2005.

Product may be purchased by visiting
www.gloriamorrow.com.